FROM MOTHS TO MERLINS

RAF WEST MALLING
PREMIER NIGHT FIGHTER STATION

*Of all the airfield in Great Britain, here, many say
(including myself) we have the most pleasant.*

Guy Gibson whilst serving at
West Malling — 1941–2

Above: Learning to fly at Maidstone Airport. *Kent Messenger*
Below: A De Havilland Mosquito of 25 Squadron sits in front of the West Malling tower
c. 1944. *RAF Museum via R. J. Brooks*

FROM MOTHS TO MERLINS

RAF WEST MALLING
PREMIER NIGHT FIGHTER STATION

ROBIN BROOKS

FONTHILL

Fonthill Media Limited
www.fonthillmedia.com
office@fonthillmedia.com

First published in the United Kingdom 2013

British Library Cataloguing in Publication Data:
A catalogue record for this book is available from the British Library

ISBN 978-1-78155-335-0

Typeset in 10pt on 13pt Sabon LT
Printed and bound in England

Connect with us
 facebook.com/fonthillmedia   twitter.com/fonthillmedia

Contents

Above: A Moth from West Malling lands short of the airfield and rests in a hop field.
Below: A Dudley-Watt DW1 which was based at West Malling, 1935. *Real Photos*

INTRODUCTION

As a flying club airfield during the 1930s, West Malling was well known and very popular. 1939 saw it requisitioned by the military and it became a forward landing ground to Biggin Hill and Kenley. Though out of use during the Battle of Britain due to non-completion of the building work, and heavy bombing by the Luftwaffe, from 1941 onwards it became the premier night-fighter station in No. 11 Group, Fighter Command. During the Dieppe operation the airfield was used by day fighter squadrons and in 1944 became the main anti-diver airfield for the aerial destruction of the V1 Flying Bomb. In peace it continued the night defence of our country until the RAF left in 1960.

An American Naval Facility Flight moved in shortly after and stayed for two years before moving to Blackbushe airfield. No. 618 Volunteer Gliding School continued to give air experience and gliding licence flights to Air Cadets together with Metair Aircraft Equipment Ltd who arrived to fit out and test the Saab/Fairchild 340 aircraft.

When Kent County Council purchased the airfield from the Ministry of Defence in 1970 it was hoped that the airfield would remain flying when they stated that 'they had acquired the airfield to prevent it from undesirable development'. Sadly this is exactly what did happen as the flying elements were forced to leave and the airfield became destined to become a scientific and technical park surrounded by thousands of houses.

Today it is not recognisable that the site was ever an airfield, but I hope that this history of West Malling will mean that it is never forgotten. I dedicate the following chapters of history to all those men and women, military and civilian, who lost their lives or were injured whilst serving at Royal Air Force West Malling.

Robin J. Brooks

Above and below: The start of a day's flying at West Malling, 1935.

CHAPTER 1

IN THE BEGINNING

By 1918 aviation had grown into an important industry. The military value of the aeroplane had been recognised by some at the start of the Great War and its usefulness rapidly increased throughout the four years of war as progress in design and engine power gathered pace. With the signing of the Armistice, the situation changed almost overnight. The cancellation of military contracts was devastating and many well-known aviation firms were forced to close. Convinced that the aeroplane was a weapon only with the ability to kill and destroy, the public was not yet ready to fly.

Despite the cessation of hostilities, civil flying was not permitted in Britain until 1st May 1919. At first it was commercial airline companies that led the way. The period from 1919 to the end of the 1920s became known as the era of great flights. In parallel with the development of commercial aviation, private flying began to grow, albeit rather slowly. Only when De Havilland produced their Moth biplane did a new enthusiasm arise and this spread like magic throughout the British aircraft Industry. It made possible the flying club movement and led to the expansion of the industry across the British Empire.

For the town of West Malling, the year of 1929 was of significance due to the arrival of electricity in the area. South of the town, where the road led to Mereworth, there was an area known as Kingshill and it was here that some 100 acres of green grassland had been designated a war-time landing ground for aircraft stationed at Detling. Being on high ground, Detling was often subjected to low hill fog and aircraft would divert to this emergency strip at Kingshill. From 1918 it had become virtually deserted and overgrown and it was assumed by the village people to have been forgotten. But not entirely so, for by 1930, with the rekindled interest in private aviation, people were again looking at potential flying sites. Mr P. H. Meadway, who owned a company called Kent Aircraft Services, was one interested person, for he had recently received notice to vacate his premises at the little airfield at Penshurst due to its premature closure.

MAIDSTONE

1. Controlling Authority.—Malling Aviation Ltd., Maidstone Aerodrome, Kent.

2. Landing Area

(*a*) *Dimensions.*—

N.—S.	700 yards.
N.E.—S.W.	850 yards.
E.—W.	720 yards.
S.E.—N.W.	800 yards.

(*b*) *Altitude above Mean Sea Level.*—280 feet (85 metres).

(*c*) *Surface conditions.*—Grass covered. Slight slope down towards the N. An area in the S.E. corner is at present unsuitable for landings and is temporarily fenced off.

3. Obstructions Requiring Special Caution.—Nil.

4. Special Signals.—Nil.

5. Lighting

(1) *Beacon.*—

(*a*) *When operated.*—Irregular. (Under R.A.F. control.)

(*b*) *Character and period.*—Red, flashing the Morse letters M E (— — •) approximately every 10 seconds.

(*c*) *Normal range.*—7 miles.

(*d*) *Situation.*—Mobile.

(*e*) *Overall height.*—(i) *Above ground level :* 5 feet (1·5 metres). (ii) *Above sea level :* 285 feet (87 metres).

(2) *Landing lights.*—Flares will be displayed provided that 48 hours' notice is given.

6. Facilities for Aircraft

(1) *Refuelling.*—Aviation fuel, oil and fresh water available. Refuelling pumps installed.

(2) *Repairs.*—All repairs can be executed.

(3) *Hangars.*—

Number.	Structure.	Net. Breadth.		Net Depth.		Door Height.		Door Width.	
		ft.	in.	ft.	in.	ft.	in.	ft.	in.
One	Steel and asbestos	75	0	60	0	15	0	75	0
One	Steel and wood	40	0	72	0	10	0	30	0
Three ..	Wood (lock-ups)	15	0	36	0	10	0	15	0

The locality of Kingshill was known to him and it was on a Sunday in April 1930 that he chose to inspect it. He found that it was perfect for his operation and by June he had completed the necessary legal requirements to enable him to set up his business there. Erecting a wooden clubhouse and a canvas hangar beside the 'Sportsman Inn', whose gardens backed onto the airfield, Mr Meadway named his company Kent Aeronautical Services. He had assembled quite a collection of aircraft including several Avro 504 k's and a modified SE 5A. This latter he called a Dudley Watt DW1 whilst his own personal mount was an Avro 504 k registration G-AAWC. He founded the West Kent Aero Club on his arrival at the airfield, taking on the job of secretary himself, and he announced that from henceforth Kingshill would be known as West Malling airfield.

It was not, however, only powered flight that was to occupy the airfield during its infancy. Gliding had by 1930 become very prominent in the race to prove that human flight in a heavier-than-air machine was possible. In Kent it had arrived in earnest by the courtesy of Mr 'Jimmy' C. H. Lowe-Wylde. He had been a disciple of the Scotsman Percy Pilcher who had designed and built a series of Lillienthal type gliders and when Pilcher conducted further gliding experiments at Eynsford, it was Lowe-Wylde who was always there to assist. By 1930, he was experimenting with his own gliders and had established a workshop behind the 'Nags Head' public house in Maidstone. On 23 February 1930, a glider aptly named 'Columbus' was loaded very carefully onto a trailer and taken up to Detling airfield. After several attempts it flew and Lowe-Wylde had proved that it was not necessary to import continental machines for the many gliding clubs that were coming into existence. Finding the 'Nags Head' a little restricted for room, Jimmy Lowe-Wylde transferred his operation, by now called the British Aircraft Construction Company, to a purpose-built factory in part of the Isherwood-Foster's brewery at Maidstone. Between 1930 and 1933, two seat gliders were developed and work had started on a powered version of the sailplane. Called the 'Planette' lightaircraft, it was powered by a 600cc Douglas motorcycle engine mounted as a pusher above the wings. Lowe-Wylde constructed four of these machines and it was whilst flying one of them from West Malling that he became ill in the air and crashed to his death on 13 March 1933.

C. H. Lowe-Wylde had brought gliding within the reach of the people and, had it not been for his untimely death, he would have figured prominently in the expansion period of private flying. A Sopwith Dove owned by Lowe-Wylde was abandoned at the airfield after his death, but it eventually came into the hands of Mr R. O. Shuttleworth who, in 1937, rebuilt it as a Pup.

West Malling as it was in the age of Malling Aero Club. Pictured on the grass are two De Havilland Moths. *Aerofilms*

In 1931 Jane's *All the World's Aircraft* recognised the existence of West Malling as it categorised the airfield under the label of Light Aeroplane Clubs and named Mr P. H. Meadway as secretary. It was now becoming a field of some significance and, as such, began to play host to many of the air displays and pageants that were touring the country. Saturday 12 April 1931 saw the first of many when Captain C. Barnard arrived with his 'spectacular'. Well, it actually consisted of only one aircraft, a Fokker VIIA, but the people who flocked to the airfield were well satisfied with what they saw. In 1932 Alan Cobham brought his flying circus to show for two days and managed to thrill the people even more when one of his Avro 504's crashed in some woodland to the North of the airfield. Together with flour bombing, balloon bursting and the 5s joy ride, Cobham did much to ensure that light aviation was here to stay.

All of this could not, however, prevent Mr Meadway from becoming an early victim of inflation. He gradually used all his resources and capital until, in July 1932, he realised that he could go no further and reluctantly put the airfield and its buildings up for sale. By the end of the month it had been sold for £4,250 to a company called Land, Air and Water Services Ltd, owned by a gentleman with the improbable title of Count Johnston Noad!

'Jimmy' Lowe-Wylde on an early BAC glider. This was built at Maidstone and was flown regularly from West Malling. *KAHRS*

As befitted the title, the Count was a very flamboyant character who always sported a monocle, black velvet cape and ebony walking stick. He was a former motor boat racer and gave the impression of being extremely wealthy and a man about town. From his company he formed a parent company called Maidstone Airport which he owned in partnership with Mr John Amery. The little grass airfield was duly christened when the word Maidstone was written in chalk beside the compass circle and the company began operating with two De Havilland 60 Moths that had been acquired from Mr Meadway, the former owner. G-ABPK and G-ABAI were used for flying instruction under the watchful eye of the Chief Flying Instructor, R. F. Bulstrode.

In order that he should make a profit from the airfield, Count Johnston Noad organised far more than pleasure flying and the airfield became the venue for car racing, clay pigeon shooting and a great deal of socialising. The Count also had a flair for drama, leading him to organise a series of 'at home' days at the aerodrome. The highlight of these occasions was the fake runaway of a DH Moth which was performed by the Count and Mr Bulstrode. With Noad himself playing the mechanic, he would be seen to be swinging the propeller on the Moth which to all the onlookers appeared not

The Avro 504 which overshot the airfield during Alan Cobham's display in April 1932. *B. K. King*

to have a pilot in the cockpit. Suddenly the engine would burst into life and the aircraft would begin to taxi somewhat haphazardly before eventually taking off, still with no visible pilot, but with the Count chasing after it. Turning about, the Moth would make a very erratic dive towards the crowd line, pulling up above their heads, making two circuits of the field and finally landing rather heavily, with the pilot now in full view. It certainly fooled the people as amidst loud cheers and much hand clapping, Mr Bulstrode jumped from the aircraft and ceremoniously bowed to his appreciative audience.

Unknown to the majority of people, however, was the fact that despite his impressive title, the Count was inadequately financed. When he first acquired the airfield he noticed that around the perimeter there were several cottages. These were on the adjoining land that was owned by a farmer with the name of Cronk. Wishing to impress the local community, the Count employed a chauffeur and he approached Mr Cronk with a view to renting one of the cottages for the man. Wishing to assist a new business in the area, Mr Cronk agreed but very soon the rent began to fall into arrears. Undeterred by many requests for the money to be paid, Count Johnston Noad asked Mr Cronk about the long grass growing on the airfield, could he help by cutting it? Mr Cronk agreed to cut it free providing he could stack the resultant hay in

Gypsy Moth of West Malling Aero Club in one of the hangars. Behind it is a damaged Belgian Tipsy.

DH 80A Gypsy III of Malling Aero Club. *R. Riding*

a corner of the field for removal and use during the winter. It was duly cut and stacked and nothing more was thought of it. Some time later when Mr Cronk decided to use some of it for his animals, he found that it was not there and learned from another source that the Count had actually sold it to another farmer! Not being able to confront Johnston Noad personally due to the fact that he was always out (!) Mr Cronk went to the chauffeur's cottage and mentioned the fact of the hay and the rent arrears. The chauffeur replied that he was not surprised as he and the rest of the employees had not received any wages for some months. It cost the local trades people in the village and Mr Cronk dearly, although the daily scandals about the Count and his friends livened the country village atmosphere.

By December 1932 the airfield was again in financial trouble with the only answer being to close the Maidstone Airport enterprise but retain the Land, Air and Water Services. Almost immediately the prospects appeared a little improved and by April 1933 with Alan Cobham's flying circus again the star attraction, things began to pick up for the Count. 22 July 1933 was the occasion when the airfield was officially opened and named Maidstone Airport yet again. A grand ceremony and display was organised with flypasts by Vickers Virginias of 500 (County of Kent) Squadron which was stationed at Manston. By now, Count Johnston Noad was proclaiming Maidstone Airport to be the commercial airport of the world stating that it was a far better site than Croydon, then the international airport in Britain. All of this, however, fell on deaf ears or, perhaps, the public had seen enough of the Count and his daydreams. By January 1934 he had reached the end of the road and was declared bankrupt. The airfield reverted back to West Malling aerodrome and a few months later was sold for £6,000 to a company calling themselves Malling Aviation. As a rather seedy era closed for the airfield, so a new bright and prosperous age began.

It fell to Malling aviation to reinstate the airfield as a place for serious flying and good socialising. Jane's 'All the World's Aircraft' stated under the heading 'Light Aeroplane Clubs' Malling Aero Club, West Malling Kent. The British Civil Register mentioned that the company owned several De Havilland 60G Moths, and at least one Hawker Tomtit G-AALL which was an ex-Prince of Wales' King's Cup entrant. The part owner and secretary was a Mr Walter Laidlaw and it was mainly under his direction that the club flourished. Himself the owner of a 'Pou de Ciel' or 'Flying Flea', the club actually had seven 60G Moths on strength, G-AACZ, G-AAFD, G-ABYZ, G-ABAM, G-ABWN, G-ABLH and G-AFTG.

Mr Laidlaw managed to bring a very different tone to the airfield than that set by his predecessor. His wife was American and she managed to

Part of Malling Aero Club's fleet of DH Gypsy Moths. *R. Riding*

introduce some unusual transatlantic dishes which at this period were very unfamiliar. The clubhouse began to be used not only by flyers, but by local doctors, farmers and businessmen who wanted to eat and drink somewhere intimate with good food being served. Mrs Laidlaw also ran the office and was the general secretary, her daughter, Babs, eventually managing to make it a complete family affair by keeping the flying accounts at the weekends.

By 1935 Malling Aviation had taken the lease on the airfield and it had become known and registered as Malling Aero Club. The usual round of air displays were again including West Malling in their yearly itineraries, beginning with the flying circus of Alan Cobham who gave a display on 3rd July of that year. Walter Laidlaw was still building his 'Flying Flea' in one of the hangars and, fitted with a recently-acquired Anzani engine, it was ready for its first flight by the end of the year.

In 1936 the Malling Aero Club could boast fifty members, although not all of them flew. Those that did usually carried out about twenty-seven hours total flying time before being given their 'A' licence. Fifteen of these hours had to be solo flights. The acquisition of the licence authorised pilots to fly any type of land-based plane and with the club having several instructors

Two photographs of T. Campbell Black's air display at West Malling in 1936. *B. K. King*

including Mr Laidlaw, it became commonplace for the residents of Malling village and the surrounding area to have their doubts about the confidence of many of the pupils. The Chief Instructor was Mr George Goodhew and it was he that had the unenviable task of deciding whether or not a pupil was qualified enough to hold a licence.

As the year drew to a close, Malling Aero Club looked to the market for more aircraft and the addition of a Southern Martlett (G-AAYX) was a sign of expansion within the club. Facilities were by now extended to two hangars and a clubhouse, all of this proving such an attraction that by Christmas a halt to membership had to be called, so great was the demand for flying instruction. The year had been a success for Walter Laidlaw with air displays by Alan Cobham and T. Campbell Black proving very popular. With the arrival of a company called Plane Advertising the lease of a further field was necessitated, and the future appeared very promising.

In those halcyon days flying competitions were part of the fun and, in 1936, one of these was held to find the club member best able to land his aircraft in a given time and space. The competition would begin by individual aircraft taking off, flying a set course in a certain time and landing back at Malling, all within the stated time and distance. Competition was very fierce and the first year it was won by the Chief Instructor George Goodhew. With the cup duly engraved, he kept it for the rest of the year and in 1937, handed it over to the new winner who was Mr Ken Vinson, another club member.

The Tipsy being broken up in the club hangar. *KAHRS*

Gypsy Moth with Dr W. Van Essen, a member of the flying club, in the rear cockpit. *Dr Van Essen*

Hawker Tomtit G-AALL of the flying club in flight. *Dr Van Essen*

He owned a very sporty single seater aircraft which he vulgarly named 'Hoof-hearted'. His fiancée, however, did not share his love of flying and insisted that he gave it up before she would agree to marry him. Reluctantly, and with his name engraved on the silver cup for posterity, he did. Whether or not they lived happily ever after is not recorded!

The 1938 competition was won by Mr R. Compton-Hall and sadly this was to be the last year of the event as the clouds of war began to gather. Another year was to pass before civil flying for pleasure was ordered to stop and the flying clubs, including Malling, made the most of what now appeared to everyone to be the last year of peace.

On 10 December 1937, the very lovely Hawker Tomtit (G-AALL) that Malling Aero Club owned was involved in a taxiing accident and had to be scrapped. It happened on the very day that Amy Johnson chose to fly from the airfield and, being a plane beloved by all the members, it was sad to see it demolished.

During the last year of peace, many other aviation personalities flew from Malling. They included Pauline Gower, Betty Sayers and Jean Batten. It was the latter pioneer who kept her aircraft, in which she had flown to New Zealand, in one of the hangars at the airfield.

One member of the Laidlaws not mentioned so far was the family dog, a big ugly Bull Terrier. He could always be seen loping around the club house

The landing contest cup so valiantly sought after by members of the Malling Aero Club. *G. Cardew*

The Royal Engineers often held 'At Home' days at West Malling. Pictured is a Fury of the Royal Engineers Flying Club. *Royal Engineers*

Type 639 Cadet at West Malling. *Dr Van Essen*

but, of course, was never allowed to stray onto the grass field. Usually he would just lie outside the clubhouse soaking up the sun whilst the club activities went on around him. The instructors at Malling Aero Club did not stick rigidly to any particular aircraft whilst flying, taking any machine that happened to be available at the time. Strange to say, the dog always knew which aircraft Mr Laidlaw was flying, even when he landed at the far end of the field. He seemed to ignore all the other aircraft in the circuit until the particular aircraft that contained his master went overhead or landed. He would then rise to his feet, yawn and begin barking, wagging his tail in anticipation of a friendly pat from Mr Laidlaw. It was a most uncanny experience and made everyone realise that the dog had great intelligence after all. However, one of Bobby's less likeable habits was his love of everything and anything that stood still long enough for him to perform a necessary function by raising either of his hind legs. New club members standing talking and not noticing his approach would suddenly be aware of a wet feeling around the ankles, the older members knew they had to keep on the move and avoided standing still for too long.

It was this happy atmosphere of flying that had to end in 1939. West Malling had already received a visit from the Directorate of Public Works prior to a Royal Air Force station headquarters being set up. When the final notice of possession was handed to Mr Laidlaw, it was with a sad heart that he prepared to leave the flying club and disband Malling Aviation. Taking his personal belongings with him he closed the club house for the last time and gave the keys to the RAF Officer in charge of West Malling, the family finally emigrating to the Virgin Isles. The war meant the end of Malling Aero Club and it was never again to be reinstated. Those halcyon days of flying are memories to the many aviators who gained their pilot's licence at Malling, for the war had finally arrived and Malling airfield was to play a very prominent part in it.

CHAPTER 2

INTO WAR 1939-40

The expansion of West Malling began rapidly with the setting up of a station headquarters. By early 1939, the builders had extended the airfield and had constructed permanent brick buildings for the airmen. Two grass runways were laid and strengthened with Sommerfeld track to ensure all-weather serviceability and a watch tower and office was installed to give airfield control. West Malling was ready to go to war from the onset in 1939, but it was to endure a very phoney period before it actually saw battle.

By early 1940 the airfield defences had been built and were manned by units of the Army. Two Pickett/Hamilton retractable forts had been placed alongside both runways in case an airborne invasion of the airfields took place and the nursing staff of No. 4 Casualty Clearing Station were in attendance in their new hutted hospital, but as yet no aircraft had been seen at West Malling. Designated as a satellite of Kenley and a forward landing ground for Biggin Hill and Kenley, the airfield came under the umbrella of No. 11 Group Fighter Command and together with Biggin Hill, Gravesend, Hawkinge, Kenley, Manston and Lympne, was to bear the brunt of the ensuing battle. By May 1940 the grass airfield measured 1,100 yards north-east to south-west, 1,300 yards south-east to north-west, 1,200 yards north to south and 1,400 yards east to west. The north to south landing area was later extended to 1,666 yards and the main east to west runway was extended by 760 yards. In addition, one J-type hangar and several blister hangars were erected around the perimeter, these in the main being hidden by an abundance of trees that surrounded the airfield.

It was not until 20th June that a resident unit became established at West Malling and on that day No. 26 (Army Co-operation) Squadron flew their Westland Lysanders from Lympne, from where they had been operating over the Dunkirk beaches dropping food and water supplies to the beleaguered Army below. Their task at Malling was to pinpoint leaks in the night black-out within the area and to assist the local ack-ack units in reconnaissance and photographic sorties, all of which they found very boring.

The trails of a dogfight high above Kent. *Kent Messenger*

The ground and aircrews were billeted in the new hospital huts on arrival and the officers were accommodated some distance from the airfield at a lovely old grange that had been requisitioned by the Air Ministry and was known as the Manor House.

It was during July of that year that official orders were received stating that all aircrew personnel were to be of at least Non-Commissioned Officer rank. Prior to this, some of the flying personnel were of airman ranks (i.e. Leading Aircraftsman etc.) but it was felt by the Air Ministry that these airmen should carry the rank of Sergeant or higher. On the evening of the official announcement the bar at the 'Rose and Crown' in West Malling High Street was crowded as usual with 26 Squadron, but this sudden rise in many of the airmen's rank (and pay) led to an excessive celebration. Towards closing time, someone produced his Colt 45 (this was standard issue to aircrew at this time) and two 45 bullets found their way into the ceiling of the bar. The same exuberance continued in the Wild West type battle which continued along the main street and all the way back to camp. Noticeably there were a few bad heads next morning!

Although by this time the Battle of Britain was being fought in the air above Kent and Sussex, no call was made upon West Malling to accommodate any of the squadrons active in this particular battle, despite the present-day myth that West Malling was a Battle of Britain airfield. Historians define the Battle as being from 10 July to 31 October 1940 and between these dates not one Hurricane or Spitfire Squadron flew from the airfield, though some used it as an emergency landing ground. It was still 26 which was the resident operational squadron.

The period running up to the battle was known as the 'Phoney' War: the predicted invasion of the British Isles had not materialised and contact with the enemy was non-existent. This was, however, also a period in which to take stock of our very weak home defences and in this respect, 26 Squadron could be counted among the forerunners.

When the squadron arrived at West Malling a standing list of orders was published, a copy of which was displayed in every section. It mentioned that if the air raid siren sounded during the night, the men were to make their way to the casualty clearing station, thence out of the main entrance, down the road turning right about opposite the 'Bell' public house and so to the outer edge of the airfield where the armament section of the squadron had established a twin Lewis gun defence point. It was most fortunate for them that the 'Bell' was only a few hundred yards from the site, with the landlord only too willing to increase his takings by wheeling the orders to the gun site on his bicycle and trailer!

The armament section was also charged with the production of Molotov cocktails as an aid to airfield defences. This duty (!) was bestowed on them with the understanding that, when the enemy tanks arrived, the best way for the squadron to destroy them was to clamber onto the tanks, raise the lid and drop this lethal beer bottle into the tank. Others were instructed to place these same home-made bombs into the paths of the tank tracks, though just how they were supposed to disguise themselves as cow manure laying in the grass was never worked out. However it was suggested by some of the squadron that certain ground staff began with a distinct advantage!

In June 1940 26 were joined by No. 51 wing for engineering work and Flight Lieutenant V. Mercer-Smith was posted in as Station Commander, but still no fighter squadron had arrived to aid the air battle. 26 Squadron was still carrying out reconnaissance and photographic sorties and this pattern was to continue until July when the airfield witnessed the arrival of 141 Squadron.

Flying-in from Turnhouse in Scotland on the morning of 12 July, Squadron Leader Richardson brought his Boulton Paul Defiants south to do

The fuselage of a Junkers 88 lies in the garden of a house in the Tonbridge Road, Maidstone on the night of 17 September 1940. It was attacked by Defiants of B Flight of 141 Squadron Biggin Hill and the West Malling airfield ack-ack battery. The crew of the aircraft are buried at Maidstone Cemetery. *Kent Messenger*

battle with the enemy. The Defiant had introduced a new tactical concept in two seat fighters whereby no forward armament was carried. All offensive power was concentrated in the rear cockpit by a four gun power-operated turret. No. 262 Squadron had taken the aircraft into action for the first time flying from Manston on 12 May 1940 and had found that the turret paid handsome dividends. On 29 May the squadron destroyed thirty-seven enemy aircraft in one operation, the Germans mistakenly identifying the Defiants as Hurricanes and diving on their supposedly defenceless tails. By 31 May, Defiants had shot down sixty-five of the enemy and the aircraft was deemed to be infallible.

It was with this happy situation that 141 joined 26 Squadron at West Malling. Upon arrival, the aircraft were dispersed among the trees as the Officers and men were allocated billets. Operational training began almost immediately and the squadron carried out many interception practise sorties with 26.

They had not yet flown the Defiant operationally, but by 18 July, they were deemed ready for operations from West Malling, the first 'scramble' for the squadron coming the next day, a Friday. It was an interception patrol over the Channel and, full of confidence, the pilots and gunners lifted the aircraft from West Malling at 10.45 and flew to the forward airfield at Hawkinge. At 12.15 they crossed the coastline at Folkestone to begin their patrol. There was a considerable amount of British shipping in the Channel, bait enough to bring the enemy Messerschmitt fighters and bombers up from their French airfields. Sure enough, ten minutes after taking up their position above a convoy, twenty Bf 109s were seen approaching, not in their usual position of being able to dive on the British aircraft, but slightly lower than 141, thus enabling them to climb and shoot at the belly of the Defiants. This was the unprotected area of the aircraft for the turret could not move sufficiently for the gunner to fire down on the enemy. Since the last contact with the Defiants, the Germans had realised that the safest place to be was under the aircraft enabling them to fire at will into the Defiant. The crews of 141 fought valiantly, but within five minutes six of them had been lost, shot down by the Bf 109s of 111/ 3G51. Defiants L7001, L7009, L6974, L6995, L7015 and L7016 were lost in the Channel waters, L6983 although badly hit, making it back to Hawkinge. Nine aircrew were lost with several others badly injured, most of the latter being rescued from the sea. It was a bad day for 141 and the incident made sure that the Defiant was never again used for daytime fighter operations.

The next day the remainder of the squadron were posted to Prestwick and the airfield again became home solely to 26 Squadron. By the end of July, the enemy was sending superior numbers of fighters and bombers over to attack the airfields prior to a planned invasion of England and it was not long before West Malling received their attention.

August came and the sun heralded the promise of a hot summer. At 07.30 hours on Saturday 8 August 1940 a Dornier 17 flew low over the coast at Deal and continuing inland, flew over West Malling dropping its bombs haphazardly. No warning of attack was given as the aircraft emerged from heavy cloud carrying out two runs and dropping fourteen bombs on the airfield. Many fell on the new buildings and seventeen workmen were injured by flying splinters. Three Royal Engineer sappers received minor injuries when one bomb fell directly on the building that they were occupying and two Lysanders of 26 Squadron were damaged by machine gun fire and flying debris. The Dornier was attacked by the ground defence guns, firing 175 rounds in all, but no hits on the aircraft were recorded as the pilot quickly headed for the safety of the cloud. The attack lasted about three minutes, but the trail of devastation it left behind was intense.

66 Squadron at the
Officers' Mess at the
Hermitage.
Wing Commander 'Dizzy'
Allan

The job of clearance began immediately, every available man being given orders to assist in the clean-up. Work carried on throughout the night and by the next morning, the airfield was again operational.

13 August, forever known as 'Eagle Day', was the date set by the German Luftwaffe for the defeating, crushing onslaught on the airfields in the South East. Whilst the sector stations of Biggin Hill and Kenley were bombed heavily, West Malling was not attacked again until two days later, even this being a mishap by the Luftwaffe. At 18.15 hours on the evening of the 15th, over seventy aircraft were plotted crossing the Channel after forming up over Calais. As the enemy formation crossed the coast, it was attacked by 501 Squadron operating from Gravesend, causing the Germans to split into two sections. Missing the primary targets of Biggin and Kenley, the latter formation spotted West Malling from a high altitude and released their bombs on what they assumed was Biggin Hill. Considerable damage was done to the new buildings and two airmen were sadly killed by flying splinters. An ambulance received a direct hit as it was waiting outside the new sick quarters and the same bomb blew-in all the windows and doors of the hospital. Again, all non-essential duty personnel were put to the task of clearing up, but as Friday the 16th dawned bright and sunny, the Luftwaffe returned.

At 11.00 hours the next morning, some eighteen bombers appeared over the Southern end of the airfield as clearance of the previous raids was still taking place. Dropping high explosive and incendiary bombs, they scored

The Hermitage photographed in the late 1980s. *Author*

a direct hit on one Lysander and badly damaged two more, this being the first bad damage sustained by the aircraft of 26 Squadron. One of the blister hangars was also badly hit, but no loss of life was recorded in the raid. It did, however, put the airfield out of operational use for four days.

The next day was quiet for West Malling, allowing the task of reconstruction to take place unhindered. Telephone lines to Kenley and Biggin Hill were restored, but communication with headquarters No. 11 Group at Bentley Priory was to take some time, all messages being passed via the sector stations at this time.

18 August again dawned fine and sunny and by 11.00 hours the radars had spotted the first big enemy formations forming over Calais. The first crossed the coast at mid-day and at 13.20 hours West Malling received a dive-bombing attack by Stukas (Junkers Ju 87s). Further blister hangars were damaged and three Lysanders were wrecked with direct hits.

By the last week in August, when the fighting was at an intense stage, No. 11 Group was very heavily engaged. Hitler had expected the air battle to be over in two to three weeks thus allowing his invasion fleet to cross the Channel. It had not happened and now Goering, Commander of the

Luftwaffe, was under pressure to clear the skies over England of the Royal Air Force. The main fighter airfields in 11 group were to suffer much punishment over the next six to eight weeks.

The next attack on West Malling came on 28 August when several bombs were dropped at night in the vicinity of the airfield. No damage was reported and the enemy aircraft turned away from the gunfire coming from the anti-aircraft units in the area.

The beginning of September found Goering within measurable distance of his goal. With Manston already out of use except for emergency landings and West Malling, Lympne and Hawkinge badly battered, the enemy had only to repeat at Tangmere and Kenley what he had done at Biggin Hill to make it impossible for the airfields south of London to be used. It was touch-and-go for Fighter Command as the onslaught continued.

On 3 September the Luftwaffe returned in force to West Malling and at 15.12 hours six enemy aircraft attacked the station. Kenley operations room had reported all clear as the aircraft came in unseen from the South East and dropped about thirty bombs. The raid, which lasted two minutes, killed one civilian workman and left the runways badly cratered. Several unexploded bombs landed among the new buildings and the parachute section was damaged.

It should be mentioned that at the time of these raids there were about a hundred civilian contractors employed at the camp. An airfield was definitely not a healthy place to be and with the punishment that West Malling had received, many were apprehensive about even turning up for work. This fear reached crisis point on 7 September when someone started the rumour that West Malling would that day be erased from the face of the earth, the consequence of which was that 80 per cent of the workforce failed to turn up that morning. Threat of no pay and the sack found them back at work the next day when the predicted raid still did not materialise.

The next three days saw sporadic bombing of the airfield, the worst day being the 10th when a bomb scored a direct hit on a gun post killing six soldiers and wounding three more of the Queen's Regiment who were on airfield defence. At this time a system of alerts had been introduced by the Air Ministry and consisted of Alert 3 — invasion likely but improbable within the next three days; Alert 2 — invasion probable within the next three days and Alert 1 — invasion imminent and likely to occur within the next three hours. Alert No. 1 came into operation from 8 September indicating the state of affairs within the country and this continued for the next four weeks.

Throughout the period, 26 Squadron had lost several aircraft and it was decided by the Air Ministry that the Lysanders should move out to Gatwick.

Though they were glad to be away from the bombing, the squadron had become very attached to West Malling and it was a sad day for many when they left.

Previous to 26 Squadron leaving, Wing Commander T. B. Prickman had succeeded Wing Commander R. Stevens as Commanding Officer of the station. In turn, he had also left, his successor being Flying Officer F. A. Lewis. He had remained for six days and was then replaced by Flight Lieutenant V. Mercer Smith who was posted in as CO. It was this Officer who was to see the airfield through this most difficult period.

There was a lull in the bombing of West Malling from 10 to 16 September, this being due to the rescheduling of the German invasion of England owing to the resistance of the RAF. Intelligence had informed Hitler that far from diminishing the strength of the RAF, the Luftwaffe had noticed a considerable increase in fighting power. For two months the enemy had used superior numbers of aircraft in the battle, but still the airfields appeared to survive. With this in mind, the German High Command voted for a change in policy, taking the brunt of the bombing away from the airfields and concentrating on London in the hope that this would force Britain to sue for peace.

As dawn broke on 15 September, now celebrated annually as Battle of Britain Day, West Malling was not on the German list of airfields to be attacked. It was the capital that became the target. The day was, however, memorable for the airfield with the landing of a German bomber. At 15.00 hours, a Heinkel He 111 flew low over the field with several Hurricanes and Spitfires in chase. It turned sharply and was forced to land on the grass, finally stopping abruptly beside one of the blister hangars. At the same time, one of the attacking Hurricanes from 238 Squadron based at Middle Wallop also had to land with engine trouble. The pilot, Flight Lieutenant M. V. Blake was unhurt and managed to jump clear of his aircraft before it caught fire on the ground. Running over to the Heinkel he arrived at the same time as the West Malling Intelligence Officer and several armed airmen. They found two of the crew, Uffz Lange and Gefr Sailor, both dead. Offering no resistance, the remaining three crew men, Uffz Zilling, Fw Beherends and Fw Lichtenhagen, gave themselves up to the Officer and were promptly marched off to the guardroom. The two dead crewmen were placed in the station mortuary to await burial the next day. It was quite a day for West Malling and although the Heinkel was classified as a write-off, it was taken to pieces and transported to Farnborough for evaluation by the scientists.

The next day, one enemy aircraft dropped its bombs in the vicinity of the airfield, but no material damage was done. Again on the 17th and 18th, single aircraft carried out attacks and although they were nuisance raids, they did no structural damage nor did they cause any loss of life. A further raid was carried out on 28 September and for several nights after, the last raid of any significance being on 18 October.

The constant bombing, however, ensured that the airfield was not serviceable for any squadron throughout September or October and by November the Battle of Britain was over. It petered-out as the Luftwaffe withdrew from the daylight assault and winter set in. Though West Malling had suffered badly from enemy bombing, it had not reached anything near its potential as a fighter airfield.

With the Battle over, its slice of the action was about to begin.

A fine photograph showing how camouflage changed the face of West Malling. *RAF Museum*

CHAPTER 3

THE REAL WAR BEGINS

It was not until 30 October 1940 that it became possible for West Malling to accept a full fighter squadron. On that day No. 66 flew in with Spitfire Mk. 1's from Gravesend, to which they had become very attached. Commanded by Squadron Leader A. S. Forbes DFC, they had achieved a magnificent record in the Battle of Britain and for them West Malling was to offer a brief respite from constant battle. Over the past two months, the squadron had suffered the turmoil of many changes of posting and to many of the men, the move to this airfield was the last straw. This was further amplified when, on landing at West Malling, three Spitfires promptly crashed, the cause being that some 'oaf' of a civil engineer had filled the bomb craters in with clay and the wheels of the aircraft, sank, causing many a bent propeller and damaged undercarriage. Those that did land safely were re-fuelled and dispersed among the trees swiftly, lest some enemy bomber should come snooping.

The Officers' Mess was a large house on the East Malling road called 'The Hermitage'. This was a rambling Kentish rag-built house and the men very soon made it all their own. The weather had clamped in with mist and heavy cloud, this in turn keeping the enemy at home as well as grounding 66 Squadron. There really was nothing to do except to eat, drink and be merry and the local public houses in the West Malling and Maidstone area were witnesses to this effect.

66 Squadron were to fly no operational sorties from the airfield for one week after their arrival, it was decided that they would be better used operating from Biggin Hill. And so another upheaval took place as the squadron departed for Biggin and once more West Malling became just a satellite airfield.

The damage from the bombing was still being repaired, albeit rather slowly. With the threat of an instant invasion by the Germans over, the workmen seemed to slow up even more. Only the threat of the station adjutant's boot being strategically placed seemed to push them into any sort of motivation.

On 31 October the field again became partially operational with the arrival of 421 Flight with Hurricanes and Spitfires. Commanded by Flight Lieutenant C. P. Green, the main function of the unit was to undertake fleet spotting duties and to act as faithful escorts to the Fairey Swordfish squadrons that were based at Manston. They remained only for a short time, for the lack of targets for the Swordfish meant that the use of front-line fighter aircraft for escort duties was not a viable proposition.

Christmas 1940 came and went and, though thick snow carpeted West Malling in January and February 1941, it was left to melt of its own accord as the airfield had once again become just a satellite.

One sign that the future use of the airfield was assured came with the construction of a public house within the security bounds of the station. It was built in seven months by Whitbread Fremlins and by December 1940 it had been officially opened. Given the name of the 'Startled Saint', it was a witty speculation on the reaction of St Leonard, who had once rested at West Malling, and his feeling should he have returned and found the airfield with its wartime takeoffs and landings. The landlady was Mrs Alice Baker and she was to remain as 'mine host' for thirty-eight years. As the Inn was within the bounds of the station, it was necessary for customers to show their identity cards to the perimeter guards before they were allowed to enter the bar. With the period known as the 'phoney war' past, invasion was still uppermost in people's minds.

In March 1941 the Cierva Autogiro (G-ACWM) came to West Malling, having been conscripted by the RAF for radar calibration work. Its task was to ensure that vital stations returned to the air after enemy attacks had disrupted communications to Fighter Command Headquarters and various sector stations. Designed by Juan de la Cierva, the autogiro first flew in January 1923. The first rotating wing aircraft, it offered hopes of improved safety by eliminating long standing and take-off runs. It was also capable of a slow speed and this was ideal for the purpose of calibration and it did, indeed, give sterling service to the RAF.

A change of command came to West Malling on 14 March 1941 when Squadron Leader V. Mercer Smith, recently promoted from Flight Lieutenant, handed over the reins to Wing Commander A. M. Wilkinson DSO. Being given the usual treatment for a departing CO, that of being towed around the base on an alien object, Squadron Leader Mercer Smith wished the airfield and his successor every success and left for pastures new.

Work continued on repairing bomb damage. New brick billets were being built and these, together with a modern brick control tower and a semi-sunk operations room built among the orchard trees, allowed West Malling

A Beaufighter of 29 Squadron airborne from West Malling. *J. Rawlings*

to look to the future with confidence. The reconstruction was finished by March, but it was not until 14 April that the station was ready to accept full squadron status. It fell to No. 264 Squadron, flying their Boulton Paul Defiant 1's across from Biggin Hill to Malling, to convert it from non-operational to operational. The Defiants, since their disastrous operations of 1940, were now flying in a night fighter role, but a single operation flying from Malling was to prove that, even in this role, it was a limited aircraft. They stayed at the base for three weeks before they received orders posting them to Colerne, away from the main battle area. Before their departure No. 29 Squadron flew in from Digby and the arrival of this squadron was to mark the beginning of a very hectic few years for the airfield.

Commanded by Wing Commander S. C. Widdows, 29 Squadron had seen action during the Battle of Britain flying from Debden in Essex. Prior to this, they had a success story dating back to the First World War when they saw action in France and Belgium. Now equipped with the powerful Bristol Beaufighter, 29 had come south to attack the enemy by night.

By 30 April the squadron had settled into West Malling. With the help of Wing Commander Wilkinson, the crew quarters were established in the old Maidstone Flying Club clubhouse, the very building that Walter Laidlaw was forced to relinquish back in 1939. 29 soon made it take on a character of its own as they attempted to give it a nightclub atmosphere. The Officers' mess was again the mansion called the 'Hermitage', last used by 66 Squadron, and the ground crews were billeted out at 'Hamptons', another mansion some distance from the airfield. The men were very enthusiastic about the whole set-up, especially when they compared it with their drab living quarters at Digby. Driving back and forth to the airfield through the country lanes and orchards of Kent was sheer delight, especially at this time of year and with the promise of a long, hot summer.

With the arrival of 29 Squadron at West Malling the station and the squadron itself was built up to full strength. Flying with 29 at this period was Flight Lieutenant Guy Gibson, who was later to achieve fame as the Leader of the Moehne and Eder dams raid. Though a bomber pilot, the Air Ministry in their wisdom had allowed him and other bomber pilots to experience operational flying from the night fighting angle in order that it might give them a greater insight to evading the German night fighters when they returned to bombing raids. For Guy Gibson, West Malling was to prove the happiest posting of his service life. Shortly after his arrival at the base he was promoted to Squadron Leader and led 'A' flight, leaving Squadron Leader Pat Maxwell to command 'B' flight.

By nightfall the entire squadron had settled in, and although operations were planned for that night, the weather took a hand and no flying was possible. At the suggestion of Gibson, the entire squadron made their way to the 'Startled Saint' which, at closing time, was still resounding to the various choruses of many well-known songs!

The next night the squadron was airborne under the control of Sandwich and Wartling ground radar stations. The Beaufighter was fitted with airborne radar but during its infancy it was to prove a little unreliable and the two-man crew of the aircraft still relied on ground radar and their own eyes for a time. As new marks of radar came along, each set proved more reliable, but in 1941 it was still early days.

For the first few nights of May it was very frustrating for the crews as they patrolled along the Sussex and Kent coasts, but on the night of the 8th it was to change. It was just after dark that the air-raid sirens began to wail on the base and the surrounding villages. The squadron was airborne a short time later and the Beaufighters were vectored to a height of 15,000 feet above Brighton. Continuing to orbit Brighton, the ground controller at Biggin Hill called the flight leader:

'Hello Bad Hat 25 (call sign for 29 Squadron). Biggin control calling. We have some customers for you. Vector 180 degrees to meet them across the Channel. Angels 12 (12,000 feet) Buster (full speed).'

One by one, the aircraft pulled out of orbit and turned onto the instructed heading. Switching on the airborne radars in the aircraft, the observers finely tuned their sets. For Guy Gibson and his observer Sergeant James, the mention of 'Bad hat 17' meant that the ground controller had a target for them. Instructed to call Kenley control, Gibson pressed a button on the side of his radio and heard the tones of the Kenley controller.

'Bad hat 17. Vector 180 degrees, they're still around you crossing the coast at Hove. Orbit and flash your weapon (switch on your airborne radar).'

Circling to the left, Sergeant James switched on his airborne radar and looked for the tell-tale blip of an aircraft on the screen.

'Any joy Bad hat 17' from Kenley.

'Nothing yet, listening out' from Gibson who a second later saw the exhaust of an aircraft ahead. At the same time, James got a contact on the set and the stalking began. Taking instructions now from James and not Kenley control, Guy Gibson got himself into an advantageous firing position. Releasing the safety catch on the column, they approached the enemy from behind. A minute later the entire Beaufighter shook with the reverberations of four cannons and six machine guns being fired simultaneously. The effect was devastating and the enemy aircraft lit up as the explosives split his tail section. Diving steeply he fell away towards the sea as Gibson brought his aircraft back over the coast. Being given another contact by Kenley, he descended to 6,000 feet as James confirmed another contact on his set. Two minutes later the enemy aircraft was in visual contact and as Gibson was preparing for another victory, the German rolled over onto his back and dived into a small village. Wondering what on earth had happened, the Beaufighter returned to West Malling and at a briefing by the Intelligence Officer next morning it was discovered that a night-fighter from Tangmere in Sussex had previously hit the second aircraft that Gibson saw, doing a fair amount of damage although it did not crash until some time later just as Gibson was about to attack it. Not totally disappointed, Guy Gibson claimed one German, bringing first blood to him and his observer and to 29 Squadron whilst operating from West Malling.

On the nights of 9 and 10 May the Malling night fighters roamed far and wide bringing victories to Flt Lt Bob Braham and Flt Lt Alan Grout. The tally of victories for the squadron began to notch up as the large-scale enemy raids began to reach a climax around 12 May 1941. On that night, 500 enemy bombers were sent over in several raids, twenty-nine were brought down by night-fighter squadrons and four by flak. The Malling squadron had its fair share of success making sure that the rafters of the 'Startled Saint' and other public houses in the village resounded to merriment when the weather closed-in the next evening.

As the pace of operations quickened, the squadron was called upon to achieve even more. In June Germany invaded Russia and for a few nights the sector was very quiet allowing crews much needed sleep. Within the week the Russians, hitherto neutral, had become Britain's allies and events again became hectic. For 29 came the new role of anti-minelayers and training for this began in earnest. For some time the enemy had been sending over aircraft, usually Heinkel 111's, to lay mines in our waters. This involved very low flying by the Luftwaffe pilot usually beneath our radar screens, dropping the mines and hurtling back across the Channel. The squadron practised low-level interception at every opportunity, sometimes flying as far as the Dutch coast in order to get maximum effective practice. A new radar station was set up on the Kent cliffs to aid the fighters and it soon proved to be dangerous for the Germans to continue the operation.

At the same time as changes were being made in the British cabinet, several were taking place at West Malling. On 14 June, the Commanding Officer of 29, S. C. Widdows, took over command of the station, he in turn being replaced in 29 by Wing Commander Colbeck-Welsh. Both Bob Braham and Guy Gibson were promoted to squadron leaders, and each was given a flight within the squadron.

The anti-mine operation got quickly under way a few days later when Braham shot down the first mine-laying Heinkel. From that time 29 went from success to success. When flying was 'scrubbed' because of bad weather, the flushes of this success showed in the round of parties that were an integral part of mess life. Even Guy Gibson's newly-acquired Labrador pup 'Nigger' joined in the melée drinking out of pint pots until he usually let himself go all over the mess carpet, whereupon he was banished for the rest of the evening. On other occasions he flew with Gibson in his Beaufighter and this would, in turn, stimulate in him a greater thirst than ever!

All the time new devices were being fitted to the aircraft to improve the killing power and the weather availability. The squadron was now helping in evaluating an instrument that would allow them to land in fog as well as having the aircraft fitted with an updated airborne radar. Operations were continuing apace but in July 1941, 29 Squadron was joined by an experimental night fighter unit at West Malling.

Formed as No. 1452 Flight and commanded by Squadron Leader J. E. Marshall DFC, the 'Turbinlite' unit began operations from the airfield on 3 July 1941. The aircraft used was the American Douglas Havoc and this was fitted with an enormous searchlight in the nose for the purpose of illuminating enemy aircraft in flight. The Havocs worked in conjunction with a fighter, the idea being that the searchlight picked out the enemy aircraft and either the Havoc or an accompanying day fighter shot it down. It was rather a wild idea and it had only limited success with the experimental unit operating from West Malling for no more than fifteen months. The first

A Turbinlite Havoc of 1452 Flight. *RAF Museum*

sorties were carried out with the Defiants of 264 Squadron, but later aircraft used included the Hurricane day fighter.

Though glad to at last have a rival unit on the airfield, 29 Squadron was still achieving the greater success against the enemy. For Squadron Leader Braham, already the holder of a DFC and Bar, came the DSO together with the award of a DFC to Flight Lieutenant Jacobs, his radar operator, for their many successes: With the end of the year in sight, the inevitable changes took place within the squadron. Guy Gibson had left 29 and returned to Bomber Command. His departure did not go unrecognised with one of the biggest parties that Maidstone and the surrounding area had ever seen starting at the Royal Star Hotel in Maidstone, the favourite of many squadrons who served at the airfield. From the Star it was a short hop over the road to the Queen's Head and, when this closed, the convoy headed for the 'Startled Saint' at West Malling. It was here that the landlady, Alice Baker, held open house for 29 Squadron and it was here that the squadron felt at home. Several of the aircrew members had pewter pots inscribed with their names hung above the bar. On the eve of Guy's departure it was well past midnight before they were finally put back above the bar and even then the party continued in the mess until the early hours.

And so came December. On the 10th of the month HMS *Prince of Wales* and HMS *Repulse* were sunk by the Japanese and the next day Germany and Italy declared war on the United States. Amongst all this bad news, Christmas Eve saw Benghazi reoccupied by British forces. The war in the air appeared to be going ever so slightly in Britain's favour as the RAF became a match for the Luftwaffe in every theatre of operations.

The old year was left behind by 29 Squadron with an indelible mark being left on one of Maidstone's traffic islands in the High Street. With the award of the DSO for Braham and a DFC for his navigator earlier in the year, a lunchtime session was hurriedly arranged for certain members of the squadron at the 'Star'. The inevitable happened. Too much alcohol was consumed and at the end of the afternoon, way after normal closing time, Bob Braham insisted on driving his own car back to West Malling. Being the worse for wear, he collided with a traffic island and was subsequently prosecuted for dangerous driving. Whilst the law punished him by a fine of £5, the damage to the island was permanent and remains to this day. It was, however, a very splendid party!

Since the autumn of 1941 29 and the Turbinlite squadron had been the only resident squadrons at the airfield. A detachment of 255 Squadron, however, then based at Coltishall in Norfolk, had also brought their Beaufighters to Malling and in company with 29, though it was rumoured that there was some rivalry between a resident squadron and just merely a detachment, they began to produce results in those long and dark Autumn and Winter evenings. It was suspected that this friendly rivalry erupted at the Royal Star on that fateful afternoon and evening!

CHAPTER 4

INTO 1942

The New Year came and was celebrated in the usual manner at West Malling. The Turbinlite squadron, was still endeavouring to carry out its duties in appalling conditions. The first tragedy had struck the squadron on 8 February 1 1941 when a Havoc 1 (B 3486) overshot the runway at the airfield and crashed into orchards, both aircrew being killed. Almost exactly one year later the second tragedy came about when a Boston 1 (BD116) crashed on landing with the loss of one crew member. This was a bad start to 1942 and with no success as yet in shooting down an enemy aircraft at night, the days seemed numbered for the Turbinlites.

For 29, 1942 meant business as usual as improved radar equipment and new techniques gave the squadron further successes: It was rumoured that they were soon to receive the new Mosquito night fighter, but for the present the Beaufighters continued to give good results.

Back in the summer of 1941, 29 had been joined by 1426 (enemy aircraft) Flight. Established to fly captured enemy aircraft, this particular flight used them in mock combat against our own squadrons, thus enabling pilots to learn valuable lessons when confronted by the real enemy. At the same time came No. 1528 (beam approach) training flight which then flew Airspeed Oxfords. This flight was an experimental unit and did invaluable service in furthering progress in ground controlled landings in bad weather. 1528 left West Malling just before Christmas 1941.

Around the airfield more permanent buildings were being built within the plum and apple orchards that surrounded the airfield, thus taking advantage of the natural camouflage. Several blister hangars had been erected around the airfield perimeter for essential maintenance of aircraft and the entire airfield settled into a routine.

It was from January 1942 that day fighters began to arrive at West Malling and thus break the dominance of the night fighters. The fighters, mainly Spitfires, came to Malling to refuel and re-arm before carrying out the arduous duties of escorting bombers which were then obeying Winston Churchill's 'set Europe alight' speech. Much of the briefing for these operations was carried out behind locked doors at the airfield, so entailing stricter security measures, much to the disgust of the resident squadrons. It did little to discourage 29 from behaving exactly as they had done before and throughout February, March and April the tally of 'kills' increased. In June, Bob Braham was delegated a new navigator and immediately went into action in the new Beaufighter now equipped with Mk. 7 AI radar. With 'Sticks' Gregory in the second seat, he shot down a Dornier 217 into the sea off Sandwich. When they came to return to West Malling, the controller told them that fog had closed in and they were to divert to Manston on the coast. Unfortunately on landing they overshot the runway and came to an abrupt halt in a ploughed field. Luckily little damage was sustained to the aircraft and both Braham and Gregory walked away unhurt.

For West Malling it was now a time of change. On 25 June 1942 the popular Wing Commander Widdows was posted and Wing Commander 'Pop' Wheeler DFC MC, a First World War veteran, assumed command of the station. One month later Wing Commander Colbeck-Welsh left 29 and was replaced by Wing Commander Cleland, another popular and likeable Commanding Officer. Previous to these two changes an important one had taken place at the airfield when it received its first permanent Hurricane squadron.

It fell to Squadron Leader E. R. Thorn DFC DFM and Bar to bring No. 32 Squadron up from Manston in May 1942. Now equipped with Hurricane 11b's and 11c's, the squadron had seen magnificent service during the Battle of Britain whilst flying from Biggin Hill, Gravesend and Manston. Since 1941 the squadron had been engaged on defensive missions, but part of their task at Malling was to train for night fighting in conjunction with 1452 Flight, now named 531 Squadron, the Turbinlite unit.

It was about this time at West Malling and all the forward aerodromes in Kent that a new air of secrecy was sensed. It was all to do with Operation 'Jubilee', the proposed Allied landings at Dieppe, and if successful, a major triumph for the Allies. It was known that the Germans would put up a stiff resistance with the use of all the air power that the Luftwaffe could manage. It was imperative for the success of the operation that the skies above Dieppe be kept clear of enemy aircraft.

By early August it was apparent that an operation of some magnitude was soon to take place as West Malling began to receive Spitfire squadrons. These were in forward preparation for the landings and on the evening of 18 August 1942 610 Squadron, commanded by the legendary 'Johnnie'

Johnson, flew into the airfield to form part of a No. 12 Group Wing, the other squadrons being 485 (New Zealand) and 411 (Canadian). The entire wing was commanded by Wing Commander P. G. Jameson DFC and all three squadrons flew Spitfire Vb's. 'Jubilee' was to take place on the 18th but, due to bad weather, was postponed for twenty-four hours. At 03.00 hours on the morning of the 19th the Malling wing was at readiness and soon left to cover the invasion. 610 were the first above Dieppe and they were to witness that eventual disaster. The squadron, together with 485 and 411, flew many patrols that day and had many encounters with Messerschmitt 109s and Focke Wulf 190s. By dawn the duties had been taken over by 32 Squadron's Hurricanes from Malling and later in the morning of the 19th the Duxford Wing of Spitfires flew in to refuel and re-arm. By 13.00 hours the last landing craft was heading back to England and the operation was deemed to be over. By nightfall the Beaufighters had taken over from the day fighters and the air battle continued well into the night. By the 20th it was all over and it was time to assess the contribution that the Malling wing had made. 411 Squadron claimed a half FW 190 destroyed with another probably destroyed and a Dornier 217 damaged. 485 had destroyed a Focke Wulf 190 with another damaged and 610 claimed one and a half FW 190s destroyed, two BF 109s probably destroyed and a Dornier 217 and three FW 190s damaged. For the wing and the station it had been most productive.

Very soon, with the landings over, the Spitfires left the airfield to the night fighters once again. For a few nights after the Dieppe operation activity increased as the enemy sent over a number of Junkers 88s to look for shipping movements in the Channel and south coast ports. This suited 29 Squadron admirably and in conjunction with the Chain Home Extra Low radar stations that were situated high on the cliffs of Kent and Sussex, 'trade' again became good for them.

For the Turbinlite squadron it appeared to be the complete opposite with June proving a devastating month for accidents. The first came on the 2nd when a Boston III (W8257) collided with its fighter aircraft, a Hurricane IIc of 32 Squadron, whilst flying in formation at night. Both aircraft crashed at East Farleigh killing all crew members. On the 21st of the month a Havoc (B3470) spun into the ground at Offham, one-and-a-half miles from the airfield, and again the crew was killed. The same night, a further Boston (W8296) crashed on a forced landing near West Malling. On this occasion, happily, the two crew members survived.

For 32 Squadron after Dieppe there was no let-up in operations as they made their presence felt with daytime intruder patrols over France; attacking railways and roads and indeed anything that moved in between. These sorties proved very successful, with pilots reporting trucks and engines destroyed, fires left burning and the consequent disruption of communications.

At the same time as Malling's day squadron was tasting success, the Mayor of Maidstone was doing something positive to mark the success that 29 Squadron had achieved by night. Upon his instigation a silver cup was appropriately inscribed and presented to 29 in recognition of their efforts in preventing many a Kent home from being destroyed. The presentation over at the official ceremony, the squadron retired to its favourite hotel and hostelry, namely the 'Star' and the 'Startled Saint' before finishing the celebrations in the mess at Addington Court, the country mansion that was home to the officers and aircrew.

During the last quarter of 1942 the enemy, in addition to sporadic raids, sent over bombers and fighter-bombers singly or in small numbers during the day, taking advantage of low cloud and poor visibility to escape attack. It was impossible for day fighters which, at that time were not equipped with radar, to find the enemy. As a result, night fighters were used for a short period, for attack by day. It did mean long duties for the Beaufighter crews of 29, but any chance to get at the Luftwaffe was welcome.

It fell to Bob Braham to make the first contact with these day attacks. 19 October proved to be a foul day with a ceiling of about 200 feet and visibility about half a mile ahead. At 10.15 hours, orders came through to scramble one Beaufighter. Immediately on leaving West Malling, Braham had to go onto instrument flying. The Chain Home Extra Low radar station at Foreness told him that a 'bandit' (an enemy aircraft) was approaching five miles ahead. 'Sticks' Gregory managed to bring Bob to a position of about 800 feet astern of the enemy, a Dornier Do 217. At a range of 600 feet, the Beaufighter attacked. The German immediately dived into cloud with Bob Braham in hot pursuit. No further contact was made, however, and with hits having been registered on the fuselage, Bob and 'Sticks' could claim a 'damaged'. It was doubtful that the Dornier ever made it home.

In September 32 left the airfield having achieved great success with the day operations. They were replaced in October by No. 486 (Royal New Zealand Air Force) Squadron who brought the unfamiliar sound of the Typhoon to the district. This 400 mph fighter had a very disappointing start in life, but went on to achieve great success. The squadron carried out offensive sweeps over France, Belgium and Holland and acquired a great reputation for their train busting activities.

One of the more devastating night attacks upon the county came when the city of Canterbury was attacked by a strong force of enemy bombers and escorts. The early evening of 31 October 1942 began quietly with not much activity in the Biggin Hill sector. About midnight a force of German bombers was tracked by radar whilst approaching the Kent coast. It was assumed that they were en route to attack London but, when just over the Kent coast, they fanned out and headed for Canterbury. 29 Squadron had been airborne since nine that evening under the control of the Chain High Extra Low station at Foreness. Though plagued by a fault in his airborne radar, Bob Braham again shot down a Dornier 217 and another crew, 'Pepper and Salt', Flying Officer Pepper and Flying Officer Toone (nicknamed Salt for obvious reasons), got another. On their second sortie that night they also shot down two other 217s much to the elation of the squadron. For this superlative performance Pepper was awarded the DFC and Salt the DFM. Two weeks later the entire squadron mourned the loss of these two men when the Beaufighter that they were testing after maintenance flew into the ground. At the hearing afterwards it was suggested that Flying Officer Pepper had tried a manoeuvre that even the forgiving Beaufighter could not take. Their loss was felt for many weeks and not even a letter from Maidstone Borough Council to 29 Squadron in appreciation of shooting down the enemy in such large numbers could dispel the gloom that everyone felt.

The arrival of Guy Gibson on a fleeting visit to his old squadron lifted spirits a little towards the end of November. Arriving in a Lancaster of 106 Squadron, of which he was now the Commanding Officer, he renewed old acquaintances and old haunts. With his ever-faithful dog Nigger flying in the Lancaster as well, he stayed for two days before leaving for his base in Lincolnshire.

With the year coming to a close, the station and its squadrons felt justly proud of their achievements. The airfield was now receiving its fair share of aircraft in distress as the bombing campaign increased. One notable incident was in late November when a Boston of 418 Squadron crash-landed on the grass and began to burn. The station fire and medical crews rushed to the assistance of the crew, the result of which was a George Medal for Flight Lieutenant J. A. Elliot, the Medical Officer at Malling, and the same for Sergeant Burrage, a soldier serving on airfield defence. Two nights later the British Empire Medal was awarded to Leading Aircraftman Laker, a ground engineer with 29 Squadron for his bravery when a Beaufighter crashed on the field.

A few weeks before Christmas, Bob Braham was posted away to command 141 Squadron. A huge party was arranged and it is rumoured that it went on for two whole days. This was further accelerated when the Commanding Officer of Malling, 'Pop' Wheeler, was granted his wish to fly again, making him the oldest pilot flying at that time.

Christmas that year was grey and wet, keeping the Luftwaffe and the RAF at home, but the war at last appeared to be going in the Allies' favour. The 8th Army had won a lasting victory in the desert and was now heading to meet up with the Anglo-American Armies in Tunis. Churchill quoted 'the turn of the tide' and at last, on land, sea and air it seemed we were winning, albeit very slowly.

Bob Braham was presented with a model Beaufighter by his ground crew as he left for his new station at Ford in Sussex. The season was celebrated in the usual style and, after lunch on Christmas day, all ranks retired to their appropriate messes and reflected on 1942. It had brought despair, but it had also brought success, especially for 29. Though they did not know it at that time, their days at West Malling were numbered.

'Bob' Braham and his navigator W. J. 'Sticks' Gregory of 141 Squadron.

CHAPTER 5

OPERATIONS CONTINUE

1943 began with the Allies achieving more success against the enemy. Almost immediately the Germans began a new campaign of bombing against England in retaliation for the bombing attacks on their capital. By day, Fortresses and Liberators escorted by Mustangs and Thunderbolts flew over Malling on their way to bomb Berlin and the large German cities. At night it was the turn of the Wellingtons and Lancasters to deliver a blow at the heart of the Third Reich.

January at West Malling found 29 still firmly in residence whilst it also saw 531, the Turbinlite squadron, disband on the 25th. With no success at all for 531 and very little for the other squadrons the colossal fatality rate became unacceptable. The station was again left with 29 who considered themselves the elder statesmen of West Malling. As if to substantiate this claim the night of the 17th and 18th January was to prove very successful for the squadron.

The early evening of the 17th was very busy within the sector with several enemy aircraft operating in the area. About 11.30 p.m. fifty Luftwaffe aircraft were approaching London as 29 Squadron were scrambled for the eighth time that night. Approaching from behind the enemy and with good visibility helping, the first contact was made by Flight Sergeant Wood of the Royal Australian Air Force and his observer Pilot Officer Slaughter. Coming up beneath the belly of the enemy aircraft, a Junkers 88, Flt Sgt Wood used up all his ammunition without the satisfaction of seeing his adversary crash, though he was seen diving away and fire coming from his underside. The next contact was by Flying Officer Musgrove and Sergeant J. Petrie who attacked a Junkers 88 sending it crashing in flames. At the same time the CO of 29, Wing Commander Wight-Boycott, with Flying Officer Sanders as observer was diverted from a night exercise over the Sussex coast to intercept a Dornier 217 which had left the main pack and was heading back home across the Channel. The CO gave the 217 a quick burst, the pilot

Wing Commander Wight-Boycott and his observer Flying Officer A. M. Sanders of 29 Squadron at West Malling during 1942-3. *IWM*

promptly losing control and diving vertically into the ground. Exhilarated by this quick success, they landed back at West Malling for refuelling and rearming. Immediately taking off again, they now pursued another Dornier 217 that the radar controller had told them was in the vicinity of Sevenoaks. With throttles at full power, Wight-Boycott climbed above the 217 and came down firing at the enemy. They had the satisfaction of seeing it crash near Westerham before another contact came on the airborne radar and the Beaufighter swung left to bring it onto an attack course. The Junkers 88 saw them coming and took evasive action. Over the Kent countryside a chase developed as the German pilot tried every manoeuvre in the book to escape the Beaufighter. At an opportune moment, Wight-Boycott gave the 88 two short bursts after which the enemy aircraft caught fire and swung away. At this point, Wight-Boycott felt distinctly ill and realised that his oxygen had accidentally been turned off during the heat of the chase.

He recovered in time to spot the Junkers 88 fleeing home over Caterham and gave chase. Attacking it from behind, the Beaufighter crew had the satisfaction of seeing it dive for the ground with the crew baling out. Now low on fuel and ammunition, Wing Commander Wight-Boycott headed back to West Malling and to a hero's welcome. News of his and Flying

Officer Sanders' success had preceded them and when they stepped down from their aircraft, tired and hungry, the Commanding Officer of Malling, 'Pop' Wheeler, was the first to congratulate them and shake their hands.

The next day the national newspapers were full of the night's exploits and the crew became national heroes. For the Germans, the raid had come decidedly unstuck, but for the CO of 29 Squadron it had earned him a DSO and for his observer, a DFC. It took a long time for the squadron to let this particular crew forget their success, but at the end of the month, Wing Commander Wight-Boycott was promoted and posted to a staff job. A huge party was held to celebrate his posting and to welcome his successor, Wing Commander Millar DFC and Bar.

It was customary at this time of the war for day fighters to use West Malling for refuelling and re-arming after a combat somewhere in Kent or Sussex. On 20 January such a refuelling operation took place for a Spitfire of 91 Squadron, then based at the forward airfield at Hawkinge. Early in 1943 the Luftwaffe were trying a new technique of sending fighter/bombers across on fast missions to drop their bombs and turn straight back for Germany. Such a mission took place on the 20th just as Squadron Leader Ray Harries of 91 was taking a well-earned lunch at West Malling's mess. With no prior warning being given, due to the enemy flying well below the radar screen, the first indication of activity was when a bomb exploded in the vicinity of West Malling. Immediately Squadron Leader Harries left his lunch, ran to his Spitfire and was airborne within minutes. The radar controller on the coast gave him his heading and with his engine on full boost he reached the Messerschmitt 109s as they were crossing the Sussex coast. Positioning himself up sun, he shot down two of the enemy and, because he had run out of ammunition, could only claim a probable for his third attack. The confrontation had taken Squadron Leader Harries out over the Channel and had only lasted five minutes though it seemed like hours. Calling West Malling he turned and headed for home, arriving back in time to continue his lunch and receive many congratulations.

The 25th saw 'Pop' Wheeler, the Station Commander, posted to another station to continue his flying. He left by the traditional method, that of being pulled out of the main gate on an ammunition trolley as Wing Commander Peter Townsend DSO, DFC was welcomed into the base as the new CO.

It seemed as though there was no stopping the success for 29 Squadron. The new CO, Wing Commander Millar, was immediately indoctrinated into night fighting when on his first operation from West Malling he shot down two Dorniers, only to realise after the second attack that he was about ten feet above the cold waters of the Channel. In the excitement of the action,

Wing Commander Wight-Boycott and members of 29 Squadron. *Kent Messenger*

he had not bothered to check on his altimeter until he had seen the second Dornier on fire.

February was a depressing month with bad weather affecting operations both for the Luftwaffe and 29 Squadron. The days were filled with practice interceptions in the training huts and aircraft maintenance, the mist and low cloud restricting any operational training. On these occasions the 'Saint' was usually full by early evening and only the call of 'last orders please' would send the airmen out into the dark night and back to the mess for a further drink. March was virtually the same, but as April came round the weather improved and the hunting became a little better. It also enticed the enemy out in their, as yet, unfamiliar fast single-seat fighter/bombers to give the RAF an unexpected bonus.

West Malling in early 1943 had one J-type and sixteen blister hangars dispersed among the trees of the perimeter. The airfield was still grass-surfaced with Sommerfeld track laid to give it all-weather serviceability and the field measured 3,300 feet North East–South West, 3,900 South East-North West, 3,600 feet North-South and 4,200 East-West. It was typical of many of the German-held French airfields and it was this fact that enticed the Luftwaffe to land at many of the Kentish airfields in error. Such an incident took place on the night of 16-17 April 1943.

Otto Bechtold's 190 in front of the tower at West Malling, April 1943. *IWM*

The station record for Royal Air Force West Malling on the 16th stated that the weather was fine and clear and very warm for the time of the year. Around midnight some enemy activity was reported by sector control at Biggin Hill, prompting the Malling controller to send a single aircraft of 29 Squadron to carry out a patrol in the Kent area. Several searchlight units were active within the area due to aircraft having been heard some time earlier; but not one searchlight had found a target. At three minutes past midnight on the 17th, a deflected searchlight beam from the Sittingbourne vicinity brought a single-engined aircraft within the Malling circuit. The duty controller thought the engine sound was that of a Defiant in trouble and ordered the airfield beacon and runway lights to be switched on. With the airfield now visible, the pilot of the aircraft switched on his own navigation lights, fired a recognition flare and turned to land on the grass runway. Completing this manoeuvre, the aircraft then turned onto the perimeter track and proceeded to make its way to the watch office beside the control tower, whereupon one of the crew of the fire tender, which was parked beside the office, jumped down and ran towards the aircraft to inform the pilot that he had landed safely at West Malling. When the pilot replied in a foreign tongue the airman realised that the aircraft was German, for the Balkan Cross was now visible on the fuselage, and ran back to the watch office for his rifle. The German pilot, however, switched off his engine and Lionel Barry of the 4th Ulster Light Ack-ack regiment went forward to help him out. No resistance was offered and Feldwebel Otto Bechtold, his arms raised in surrender, was taken into custody by the station police.

The aircraft was found to be a Focke Wulf 190 A-4 and, except for the engine cowling, was painted a sooty matt black for night camouflage. It was manhandled and placed in front of the control tower at the same time as word came through from sector that about fifteen bandits were operating in the area on fighter/bomber operations.

Twenty minutes later a searchlight beam was again deflected towards Malling and a second aircraft was heard to enter the circuit. With the runway lights still on, it too commenced a landing and had its wheels on the grass as the watch office crew took a Beaverette gun platform to head the aircraft off. When twenty yards from the aircraft it was identified as another 190, but at the same time the pilot realised his mistake and, giving his engine full throttle, he attempted to turn his aircraft around back onto the runway to enable him to take off again. Realising what was about to happen, LAC Sharlock, the gunner on the Beaverette, gave the aircraft a

The soot-like material begins to wear off. On the leading edge someone has written 'DO NOT TOUCH'. *IWM*

burst from the Vickers gun mounted on the truck, scoring several hits and causing a small fire in the back of the cockpit. One burst, however, was not enough to deter the German from taking off as the 190 continued across the grass, accompanied by a second firing from the Vickers gun. This time one of the fuel tanks was hit and flames began to envelop the entire aircraft. By now it had stopped moving and, as the Beaverette drew level, the pilot fell rather than climbed out of his cockpit, some of his outer clothing already in flames. One of the gunners from the Beaverette approached the pilot, there was a struggle and the German broke free, dodging round the back of the aircraft. Unfortunately he ran straight into the arms of the Station Commander, Peter Townsend, who had arrived at the incident some time earlier. At this point the pilot gave up the struggle and surrendered himself to the CO. He was found to be wounded in the leg and shoulders and was suffering from severe burns as the ambulance arrived to take him to the sick bay under armed escort.

By this time the aircraft was well alight and seconds later the oxygen bottles in the cockpit exploded and with them, the remainder of the fuel. With one flash the entire aircraft disintegrated and pieces of red hot metal were thrown as far as three hundred yards. Two members of the fire crew, ACI Lamb and ACI Halford, received severe injuries in their efforts to put out the fire with extinguishers, and in the ensuing explosion they were hit by flying metal and severely burned about the face and hands.

The night however was far from over as a third aircraft was heard orbiting West Malling's beacon. By now the message had spread that the airfield was being mistaken for a German base and that any aircraft within the circuit was considered to be hostile. With this assumption in mind, the RAF Regiment and the Army units who were manning the gun emplacements situated around the airfield perimeter were firing at the aircraft relentlessly. Whether they actually hit the 190 or just confused and frightened the pilot was questionable, but for whatever reason, the 190 undershot the runway and crashed into some cherry orchards just short of the threshold. Incredibly the pilot escaped with only a light fracture of the skull and lacerations as the ambulance arrived to bring him back to the station. The aircraft was a total write-off, but a guard was mounted by it for the duration of the night.

Not so fortunate, however, was the pilot of a fourth 190 which crashed at Staplehurst about the same time. First Lieutenant Kurt Klahn, realising that he was lost, left his aircraft below the permitted level, the consequence being that his parachute did not have sufficient time to fully deploy. He was found next morning by a rescue party attached to his open parachute some distance from where his aircraft crashed. The local authority informed West

Malling who sent out a party to bring the body back to the station as the parish council of Staplehurst had stated that they did not want a German buried in their churchyard. A burial service for Lieutenant Klahn was held at Barming with full military honours and he was buried in the churchyard, only later to be exhumed and re-buried in the German War Cemetery on Cannock Chase in Staffordshire.

For West Malling it seemed like a long night. No further enemy activity was apparent in the area and at 2.30 a.m. the runway lights and beacon were switched off. The 190 was placed under guard until morning and the station returned to normal status. The station diarist recorded in unexcited terms — 'an intensely interesting night'.

The next morning as the news spread throughout 11 Group that an intact 190 had landed at Malling, the station became the focus of much attention. From early morning on 17th April, a string of visitors began to arrive at the station, among the first being Group Captain 'Sailor' Malan, the Commanding Officer of Biggin Hill. Many high-ranking officers from the Air Ministry and civilian experts from Farnborough came to see the enemy and, later that evening, the 190 was flown by an RAF pilot for assessment, his verdict being that it was a very potent fighter indeed.

West Malling on the morning of the 17th was basking in warm sunshine as the airfield began to get back to normal. Parked around the airfield were many aircraft including Lancasters, Stirlings and Wellingtons, all of which had returned from raids over Germany on the previous evening and, being badly shot-up and low on fuel, could not make their home airfields. One such aircraft was a Wellington of 199 Squadron based at RAF Ingham in Lincolnshire and flown by Flight Lieutenant C. A. Bryant. The aircraft had been one of a force of 338 sent out on the first big low level raid in moonlight to Mannheim. Returning from the target, Wellington L became badly holed by ground fire and by German night fighter attacks. Losing fuel, it crossed the English coastline and the pilot, knowing West Malling to be open and operating, requested an emergency landing at the airfield. Fully explaining his position to the controller, Flt Lt Bryant was requested to join a stack 3,000 feet above the airfield due to an incident on the ground. The stack slowly decreased as prior aircraft landed and as he brought the Wellington down onto the runway the crew were amazed to see a German fighter in front of the control tower. In the pilot's own words:— 'I wondered if we had made England!'

The day of 18 April was given to the military and civilian scientists to inspect and detail the enemy aircraft and on the 19th it was flown to the Royal Aircraft Establishment at Farnborough. It was given the serial No. PE

882, was painted standard RAF green with yellow under surfaces and had a yellow P for prototype painted just ahead of the fuselage roundel.

So ended one of the more remarkable episodes at West Malling. It was later revealed that the 190 that landed and the subsequent aircraft belonged to 11/SKG 10. Each bore a yellow H aft of the Balkan Cross and a black equilateral triangle forward of the cockpit. The aircraft were from one and two Gruppen of SKG 10 and had been sent out at midnight on the 16-17 April as part of the first experimental fighter/bomber attack against Southern England, the selected targets being along the Thames and inwards to London. The 190s left the Amiens area with one 250 kg bomb and two drop fuel tanks, some of which were later discovered at Gravesend having been jettisoned on the inbound flight. The aircraft had been put on a northerly heading over Cap Griz Nez, but navigation was difficult because of ground mist and so they had become lost. In the case of Otto Bechtold, after flying on his course for forty minutes his aircraft (No. 7155) was picked up by searchlights. He released his bomb, reduced height and turned round to head back to France. After thirty minutes he saw several searchlights pointing in the same direction and, with no firing from the ground, he assumed he was over France. Following the general direction of the lights and being low on fuel, he saw the lights of an airfield and lowered his undercarriage to land, only to find himself at West Malling.

Some time later it was suggested that the 190s had been flying on a concentrated beam directed at London from France and that the 'Y' service operators at West Kingsdown near Wrotham had spoken to Bechtold in German, thereby causing him even more confusion and totally disorientating him with his position and surroundings. Whatever the reason, Otto Bechtold spent the rest of the war as a prisoner.

With the station back to normal, clearance was given to 29 to carry out intruder missions into France. This came as a welcome change from purely defensive duties and on the very first mission, Pilot Officer Cronie and his navigator Pilot Officer Colebrook shot up German barges on the Seine near the Pas de Calais, leaving them burning. Similar operations were conducted throughout the month, together with a continuance of the night operations. Peter Townsend, as CO of Malling, was very keen to see a maximum aircraft serviceability record for his station and was first to congratulate the ground crews for their unstinting efforts. It also fell to him to inform Wing Commander Millar that a signal had been received that 29 were to be posted to Bradwell Bay in Essex. It was a devastating piece of news. Surely it could not be true? Many did not want to believe it, but with forty-nine kills credited to them at West Malling, the squadron was posted with effect from

13th May. Their departure did not go unrecognised, with a farewell party at the 'Saint' continuing until the early hours. There were tears in Alice Baker's eyes as she said farewell to her beloved 'lads' in 29, for they had all shared many victories and many tragedies together. The good news was that the squadron was to convert to the De Havilland Mosquito, but even this did not entirely dispel the sorrow of leaving 'dear old Malling'.

With their departure came the end of one era, but almost immediately a new one began with the arrival of 85 Squadron commanded by Wing Commander John Cunningham, DSO, DFC, a pilot who was to achieve a certain amount of fame whilst serving at Malling.

No. 85 had previously operated from Hunsdon and, in February 1943, they had been engaged on testing a Turbinlite Mosquito, the hoped-for successor to the Havoc. It achieved no operational success and with the Turbinlite operations about to be abandoned, the squadron went over to intruder patrols with Mosquito NF XV's which were capable of flying to heights of 43,000 feet. It also flew the earlier Mosquito 12's for routine work and the squadron during its time at Hunsdon had gained a reputation comparable to that of 29. When on 10 May a signal was received notifying them of the posting to West Malling, the prospect of even better 'Hun' hunting delighted the entire squadron.

On the morning of 13 May at 09.30 hours the Mosquitoes took off and gave Hunsdon the traditional departing gesture for all squadrons, that of 'beating up' the airfield for the last time. For thirty minutes the twin Merlins of the aircraft shook the watch tower and surrounding buildings before finally leaving the airfield in silence. One hour later the airmen and much of the equipment left Hunsdon by Handley Page Harrow and the move was complete. 85 had gone south to do serious battle with the enemy.

By 10.30 that same morning the aircraft had landed safely at Malling and were busy taking over the dispersals already left by 29 Squadron. Many of the personnel came on a special train that arrived at West Malling railway station later that day. The Station Commander Peter Townsend, himself a past CO of 85, greeted them on arrival and by the late evening the unloading and billeting accommodation had been completed; 'A' flight being housed at the 'Retreat' and the 'Guest House' in West Malling and 'B' flight at 'Hamptons', a large mansion some distance from the airfield. The officers acquired a lovely house called the 'Manor House' for their own mess. Occupying high ground about five minutes from the town centre, it was a typical Georgian country house. Standing in its own grounds with a long winding drive flanked by flower borders, it had previously been used as a convalescent home for elderly ladies. Totally enclosed by walls, the front

Pilot Officer G. G. Gilling-Lax of 85 Squadron relaxes on the steps of the Manor House. He was killed whilst flying from West Malling on the night of 9 July 1943, carrying out an attack on a Dornier 217. *85 Squadron*

of the Manor opened onto a lake with ducks and swans in abundance. A list of rules which had been applicable to the convalescent home had been found by the previous RAF occupants and were on view for all to see, one of the rules stating that ladies could not be accepted as guests unless they were capable of walking upstairs without assistance. Some hope with the present occupants!

A day after 85 had arrived, Squadron Leader F. de Soomer brought the new Hawker Typhoon 1b to Malling in the form of No. 3 Squadron who were to be resident for day operations. The aircraft were a little unconventional due to the fact that they had been fitted with a bomb rack and were universally known as 'Bombphoons'. They were to operate in the fighter/bomber role, similar to the 190s that the Germans were sending over, and their brief was to hit anything that moved behind enemy lines. During the month that they flew from the base they achieved a great reputation as the 'train busters'.

With all the personnel of 85 settled into their respective billets, it did not take long for the squadron to begin operations. They were airborne by dusk on the 13th under the control of Sandwich, Wartling and Beachey Head GCI stations. They flew eight ground control interception duties that night and, although no enemy activity was found, it gave a chance for the radar controllers on the ground to get to know the new pilots now flying under their control and, of course, vice versa. It was well worth the practice for on the 16th came 85's turn to really get to grips with the enemy.

John Cunningham of 85 on the steps
of the Manor House during 1943.
85 Squadron

The sirens began to wail about 21.00 hours as the Luftwaffe 190s were
plotted crossing the Channel. At West Malling, 'B' flight were on duty and
the telephone jangling at their dispersal sent them all rushing for Mae Wests
and helmets. However, to their annoyance, it was the duty controller telling
them to stand easy as No. 3 Squadron with their Typhoons were to carry
out a patrol. Despite protests from 85, who knew that the Typhoon without
airborne radar would be useless at night, the patrol went ahead. That is,
until, with no success despite flying around in the dark for several hours,
the controller ordered them back to base and ordered off 85. It seemed as
though 'B' flight made the take-off in record time as they climbed for height
and made contact with the GCI station at Sandwich. They found the raiders
fleeing for home and, with engine boosters at full-power, one enemy fighter-
bomber was shot down near Dover within minutes of AI contact. Another
contact was picked up by Geoff Howitt and George Irving over Hastings
and as he fled across the Channel to safety they shot him down just off the
French coast, in full view of the German coastal batteries. Two shot down
and the night was still young. Another 190 was destroyed at close range
by Bernard Thwaites and Will Clemo, their Mosquito being hit by pieces
of wreckage from the 190. Just to make it a foursome, Flying Officer Shaw

A wartime photograph of the Manor House.

and Pilot Officer Lowton caught a raider near Gravesend and sent it down in flames, themselves receiving a coating of soot-like substance from the disintegrating aircraft.

It had been quite an opening night for 85. Four definites and one probable brought the congratulations pouring in, among them being one from the sector controller 'Sailor' Malan and another from 'Dingbat' Saunders, the Group controller. The night's work had ensured that 85 arrived in style. It ended at 06.00 hours on the 17th with some of the crews invading the squadron adjutant's bedroom, situated in the 'Old Parsonage' adjacent to the Manor House, with shouts of 'Yip Addy 85' and a war dance around the poor man's bed! Despite the high-jinks, it really was a job well done and it earned the squadron the honour of being the first squadron to shoot down an FW 190 at night.

The 'Wings for Victory' week in Maidstone for that week raised no less than £5,537, much of it coming from dances held at Malling. Again the squadron scored when at the Wings' dance held in the mess, the CO interrupted the proceedings with the announcement that Flying Officer Lintott and Flying Officer Gilling-Lax had just destroyed another 190. Later in the week, Wing

Commander Guy Gibson returned to his old station and took the salute at a Wings' parade for service personnel and war workers in Maidstone.

With the departure of No. 3 Squadron, 85 became the sole unit at the station. At all times, two standing patrols were maintained throughout the night, weather permitting. Two GCI stations codenamed 'Skyblue' and 'Recess', together with the new low level radar stations situated on the South Coast cliffs, controlled the Malling squadron. With a patrol airborne, the controller at the GCI station would carry out mock attacks until the 'bandits' proper came along. The aircraft would patrol just off the coast of France and the entire length of the Channel from Sussex to Hampshire. With the myth of the 190 now out of the way, the squadron looked forward to further success with the enemy.

In June the weather became idyllic for operations with long warm days and clear nights. The Officers' Mess at the Manor House became a picture as the flowers bloomed. The main idea in accommodating personnel in large country houses was to keep them safe in the event that their airfield was attacked by the enemy. With aircraft dispersed around the outer edges of the airfield and in cleared areas of orchard for protection, it made sense to keep non-flying and non-essential personnel some distance away from the airfield. Though squadrons had used the Manor House before the arrival of 85, the officers of the squadron managed to bring a new dimension to the mansion.

85 Squadron sign a drawing of the Mosquito.

As soon as the squadron became resident, part of the cellar was converted into a bar-cum-nightclub and was named the 'Twitch Inn'. It acquired an atmosphere all of its own with soft lights, secluded corners with candles and ample supplies of wines, beer and spirits. Night after night the 'Twitch' was to echo to the sounds of revelry as the thought of death in the air was forgotten for some hours. When operations were on at night, a dice was placed upon the bar. This was supposed to signify a pilot dicing with death and conversely when bad weather prevented operations, a scrubbing brush was on show to denote that the operations for the night had been 'scrubbed'. When this happened, the 'Twitch' was operational until dawn came up and the prospect of bed for a few hours drove the men to their rooms. Guest nights were frequently held at the Manor and many local dignitaries were entertained on such evenings. Lieutenant-Colonel Sir Albert Stern KBE, CMG was one local person who became a firm friend of 85 even presenting them with a silver cup on which were inscribed many squadron victories.

The Assistant Catering Officer at West Malling during 1943 was Helen Tyson, a Warrant Officer in the Women's Auxiliary Air Force. After she had finished her day's work at the station, she would cycle to the Manor House to supervise the cooking of the officers' dinner. The only other 'WAAF' allowed into the officers' domain was a girl named Nina who served behind the bar at the 'Twitch'. One of her hobbies was reading palms and this became quite a regular occurrence at the bar until one evening, whilst reading a pilot's hand, she suddenly clasped both his hands in her own and refused to carry on with the reading. Some weeks later the pilot did not come back from an operation. This was to happen a second time before it was decided that it was a bad omen to have a reading whilst on flying duties and the practice was dropped.

A regular visitor to the mess was David Langdon, the now famous cartoonist. He had at sometime been an intelligence officer with 85 Squadron and still liked to visit some of his old comrades. On the occasions that he came, he drew character cartoons of some of the officers on the hardboard panels that had been put around the walls to protect the ornate plasterwork lest the mess parties got out of hand and it was damaged. Sometime later another artist in the squadron drew frames around them and they became the centre of much attention.

During that summer of 1943, the sun shone as though everything was at peace with the world. The aircrews on duty would watch nightfall come until the darkness drove them into the crew rooms on the airfield to pass the time until they flew a sortie. Come dawn, it was a drive back to the Manor House whilst the sun was kissing the earth to herald another perfect day.

The entrance to the Twitch Inn. *Author*

Some food, a bath and then bed until the afternoon period of engine testing and the night's briefing.

For 85 Squadron, life at West Malling was very good and was to continue for some time. Frequenting the 'Twitch' bar as they did, many of the pilots wrote graffiti and messages on the ceiling of the bar. This was achieved by using burning candles to scorch a name on the plaster ceiling and, if the full ceremonial procedure was followed, the correct way was to have the candle strapped to your foot and then to be supported by your comrades in order to write your name. In one particular corner, a footprint of a WAAF was marked, but no knowledge of how this was achieved has ever been found out.

Perhaps it was Nina's.

The good fortunes of the squadron continued into June as the weather stayed hot. On 13-14 June Wing Commander Cunningham and Flight Lieutenant Rawnsley took off on patrol at 23.55 hours. It was a good night with light cloud and ten miles East of Dungeness at a height of 23,000 feet contact was made with Sandwich Radar. The Mosquito was vectored onto a heading of 330 degrees and almost immediately a contact was obtained at a range of one-and-a-half miles. The enemy aircraft was losing height gently when, with maximum boost applied, John Cunningham got a visual on the raider. With 10/10ths cloud the raider was identified as an FW 190 and, closing to 600 feet, Cunningham fired a short burst into the fuselage of the 190. Without realising

The ceiling of the Twitch Inn with its candle burn writing. *Author*

it the combat was taking place in the vicinity of West Malling and the noise of the two aircraft had brought much of the station to a halt as all eyes strained upwards to watch the fight. Another burst and the 190, with its bomb still aboard, blew up and ploughed into Wrotham Hill. The pilot, remarkably, was thrown clear of his aircraft and managed to deploy his parachute. He was picked up by a local searchlight crew and, despite a broken arm, was quite cheerful as he was taken into custody.

Landing back at base shortly after 01.00 hours, Wing Commander Cunningham and Flt Lt Rawnsley were inundated with congratulations as this 190 brought John's personal score to 17, 16 of them shot down at night. Peter Townsend himself was present when they landed, but it was obvious that he was in great pain from a wound that he had sustained in 1940. One week later he was forced to seek hospital treatment and he was advised to relinquish his command of Malling. He was succeeded by Wing Commander Norman Hayes DFC and on 26 June a mess party was held in his honour attended by the Mayor and Mayoress of Maidstone, Sir Garrard and Lady Tyrwhitt Drake, Sir Albert and Lady Stern and many other local dignitaries. Other guests included 'Sailor' Malan and Captain Balfour, the Under-Secretary of State for Air.

With the arrival of July, there came a short lull in enemy activity and everyone began to wonder just why. New AI sets had arrived for the Mosquitoes

Drawings of aircraft adorn the
walls of the Twitch. *Author*

and these were quickly fitted to improve the effectiveness of the operations.
A little later in the month the weather broke and everything was grounded
for some time. On these occasions the Manor House provided refuge for
the officers as the other local houses did for the other ranks. The garden in
front of the house was terraced and beyond that a lake with an abundance
of ducks, moorhens and swans. It was the swans that held the interest of the
crews as they attempted to get airborne under difficult conditions, the lake
being very narrow and surrounded on three sides by trees.

The misfortunes that the Germans were experiencing with their FW 190
operations became even more apparent when they projected two searchlight
beams from a point near Dunkirk. This was in order to aid the German
pilots when they were returning to France. At the same time it enabled the
night fighter squadrons to find the 190s that much easier, even though the
Mosquitoes were not yet allowed over enemy territory for fear of losing
one, thus revealing the AI secrets.

Lieutenant Colonel Sir Albert Stern KBE, CMG donates a Victory cup to 85 at the Manor House. The recipient is John 'Catseyes' Cunningham and to his right is Wing Commander Peter Townsend, the CO of West Malling.

By the middle of July the weather had once again returned to typical summer and activity began to increase. The reason behind the lull in enemy activity became obvious when on 20 July, Flight Lieutenant Nigel Bunting and his navigator Freddie French were scrambled to 20,000 feet over Dover. The GCI controller told them he had a bandit and gave the pilot a course to steer. Within minutes the navigator had got two contacts, one high and one low. Flt Lt Bunting suspected a trap and opted to go for the higher aircraft as he pulled back on his stick and climbed to 25,000 feet. Immediately the crew saw an unfamiliar outline with two bright yellow exhaust flames trailing from behind. Closing to 200 yards astern, Nigel Bunting faltered in the enemy's slipstream, but regained his position and gave the German a three-second burst. With flames streaming from his fuselage, the enemy aircraft, now identified as the new Messerschmitt 210, rolled onto its back and dived into the sea off the Suffolk coast. The aircraft was the German's answer to the Mosquito and very few had been sent over to Britain in operational conditions. Unbeknown to the crew, they were the first to shoot down such an aircraft and it gave another first to 85 Squadron.

The summer of 1943 turned out to be one of the best for some years and, as the fruit hung heavy on the trees surrounding the airfield, many of the off-duty personnel of 85 got to wandering through the orchards gorging

85 Squadron aircrew outside their dispersal in 1943.

themselves with cherries and plums. Bob Braham, who was at Malling with 29, came back on a flying visit to see his old station. Together with several Beaufighters from his own squadron, 141, he landed at Malling to refuel before taking off on an intruder mission over Germany. With the progress of the war going firmly in the Allies' favour, it was now possible for certain squadrons to carry out these missions deep in enemy territory and 85 awaited their turn with bated breath.

The Luftwaffe was still keeping up its attacks using a mixture of FW 190s ME 410s and JU 88s. The Mosquito, with its superior airborne radar, was a match for any of these aircraft and the issue of Ross night binoculars helped the airborne identification of type. July and August were good months for 85 and, having been the sole residents at Malling for some considerable time, they did not take too kindly when they heard that two Spitfire squadrons were to join the base.

4 August saw Squadron Leader W. H. Wright with 130 Squadron fly into Malling with their Spitfire V6s for offensive duties over France. The next day they were joined by 234 Squadron also flying the V6 and bringing West Malling up to the standard of a front-line day fighter station. At the same time, the airfield began to accept heavy bombers of the RAF and the USAAF. Halifax, Lancaster, Fortress and Liberator used the base as a forward airfield from which they would refuel before taking off to bomb Germany. The British bombers were faithfully escorted by 130 and 234 Squadrons whilst the Americans used the Thunderbolt for similar operations.

85 ground crew by one of the Mosquitoes.

Some members of 'B' Flight of 85 Squadron beside their dispersal. Back row:– FO Symon (Nav), FO Cleaver (Pilot), Flt Lt Molony (Adj), FO Skelton (Nav), Flt Lt Burridge (Pilot), Sqdn Ldr Gonsalves (Pilot), Sqdn Ldr Davison (Pilot), Wg Cdr Cunningham (Pilot), Captain Weisteen (Pilot), ?, ?, FO Farrell (Pilot), FO Thomas (Pilot). Front row:– FO Custance (Pilot), ?, ?, Sqdn Ldr Rawnsley (Nav).

By night it was still 85 who went in to battle as darkness fell and late summer turned to autumn. On 8 September, the day Italy surrendered, the squadron discovered that they were to be the first to receive the new mark of airborne radar, the X A1. John Cunningham and Jimmy Rawnsley got another 190, but came near to disaster themselves as pieces of the enemy aircraft entered one of the engines of the Mosquito causing engine failure. Feathering the damaged Merlin, they managed to find and land safely at West Malling though both men were taken to the sickbay for a while.

More success was scored by 85 and in particular the crew of Maguire/Lovestad began to mount a good personal score. By September, the orchards surrounding the airfield were heavy with apples and pears and the aircraft dispersals placed among them gave the squadron plenty of opportunity for a little light scrumping, though (if within reason) the local farmer did not really mind!

As the month waned and the dark nights began to close in, the Mosquitoes were fitted with the new Mark X airborne radar. A Wellington was fitted as a flying classroom and training for 85 Squadron began on the improved device during October. With operations still continuing at night, life became very hectic for the navigators of the squadron and, to crown it all, the Luftwaffe, using the advantage of longer, darker nights, increased its operations. On the night of 4 October three waves of mixed types were sent over, fifteen in the first, thirty in the second and twelve in the third. 85 was scrambled early and it soon became obvious that identification of friendly and enemy aircraft was to prove a problem with so many different types in one raid. Per Buege and Claus Bjorn, two Norwegians in the squadron, had problems in identification before attacking and damaging a 410. Tarald Weisteen and Freddie French had different problems, that of searchlight units blinding them when preparing to attack and, even worse, ground ack-ack units firing aimlessly in the middle of the battle. These were all things that the night fighter pilot had to contend with at this stage of the war and it was something that was to cause them great consternation for a long time to come.

By the autumn, John Cunningham's personal score was increasing nightly. The press of the day had made him a hero and dubbed him 'Catseyes' Cunningham, something that he personally hated. His sharpness of sight was attributed to the fact that he ate large quantities of carrots, all of which was pure fallacy, but the nickname was to remain with him for nearly all his life.

It was time for a change of Spitfires at West Malling when on 6 September, 64 flew in with their mark 'Vc's' relieving 130 and 234 Squadrons who

Group Captain A. G. Malan, D.S.O., D.F.C.,
and the Officers of the Biggin Hill Sector
request the pleasure of the Company of

Flight Lieutenant Nolany and Lady

to a Dance at Grosvenor House, Park Lane, London, W. 1.,
on Wednesday, the 9th of June, 1943,
to commemorate the shooting down of the 1,000th Hun Aircraft
by Pilots of the Sector.

9 p.m. - 3 a.m.

This invitation must be produced
to gain admission.

Biggin Hill - Gravesend - West Malling - Hawkinge - Lympne.

219

Invitation to the party celebrating the Sector's 1,000th kill. Sent to the C.O. of 85 Squadron, West Malling.

Some members of 'A' flight of 85.
L to R back row:– PO Linton (Nav), ?, Lt Lovestad (Nav), ?, Flt Sgt Misselbrook (Pilot), ?, FO Sutcliffe (Pilot), ?, ?, FO Shaw (Pilot), FO Clemo (Nav), Flt Lt Robb (Pilot).
L to R middle row:– Flt Lt Thwaites (Pilot), Sqdn Ldr Green (Pilot and Flight Commander), Flt Lt Maguire (Pilot), Captain Rad (Pilot).
L to R front row:– FO Bray (Nav), Flt Sgt Grimstone (Nav), FO Jones (Nav), FO Thomas (Pilot).

In Maidstone, the Mayor's Spitfire fund began to grow. This board was erected outside County Hall. *Kent Messenger*

departed to Catterick and Rochford respectively. One week later 64 were joined by 124 Squadron for daylight escort and offensive duties but, due to a change of policy at the Air Ministry, 64 departed after only three weeks leaving 85 to fly by night and 124 by day.

The problem of the over keen ack-ack gunners again reared its ugly head when a Norwegian pilot, Lieutenant P. Thoren, and his navigator, Pilot Officer S. P. Benge, became victims to indiscriminate firing. They had been vectored by GCI to a position near Dover where several enemy aircraft were operating. As they engaged the enemy just off the coast the Dover barrage opened up and all hell was let loose. In the ensuing battle, the raiders escaped over the Channel, but pieces of Thoren and Benge's Mosquito were later found floating in the sea with no sign of the crew.

The latter part of October saw thirteen enemy aircraft leaving France, but only eight of them crossing the English coastline, 85 seeing to it that the rest of them were at the bottom of the Channel.

Canada's third night fighter squadron in the United Kingdom was No. 410 with the motto of *Nocti Vaga* — wandering by night. They had been operating out of Coleby Grange with Beaufighters for eight months with considerable success and when, after conversion to the Mosquito, Wing Commander J. W. Reid was instructed to bring his squadron South to West Malling, it was greeted with jubilation by all members. Thus, on the morning of 2 October 1943, the squadron flew in and settled down to some good hunting. Regular night patrols began immediately and although 85 regarded them as the 'apprentice' squadron, both units treated it light heartedly and they worked in conjunction with each other very well.

In November, 96 moved from Drem to make West Malling their permanent base and with this arrival, the station was up to maximum strength and every German fighter and bomber crew was to know the words West Malling very well as the three night fighter and one day fighter squadrons did battle together.

During November the squadrons at West Malling had some uncomfortable operations when it was discovered that the Germans had fitted a rear-facing radar to some of their JU 88s. No longer was it possible to come up behind a raider without fear of being spotted. It appeared as though the enemy was again gathering strength, but great hopes were being placed on the new Mark X AI radar which was being fitted to all the Mosquitoes to counteract this new dimension.

By late 1943 it was obvious that the war would continue for at least another year. Though the Allies' success had been tremendous and the RAF was winning in the skies by night and by day, it was not to be as prophesied by so many. In November when the Russians recaptured Kiev after a bloody battle, Churchill himself said that 1944 would see the climax of the war. On the 18th of the month the RAF carried out its heaviest raid on Germany and dropped 350 4,000 lb bombs in 30 minutes. December saw the Russians advance on a wide front. The plans for an Allied landing in France during the next year were at an advanced level and Christmas was celebrated in the usual way throughout the world, everyone hoping that it would be the last Christmas of the war.

At the Manor House it was celebrated as usual, but it was also a time for remembering lost comrades and actions of great gallantry. After the practice of serving the other ranks Christmas lunch, the officers retired to the Twitch bar where the sounds of revelry continued long into the night. It had been a good year for West Malling and the squadrons that flew from the field. Would 1944 really see an end to it all?

CHAPTER 6
A NEW TYPE OF WARFARE

The New Year was bright and crisp with snow covering the airfield. This hazard did not stop operations as 124 continued to operate by day. With the motto of 'Danger is Our Opportunity' bearing results, the squadron began to 'scramble' up to 42,000 feet in order to catch the high-flying Junkers 86bs that the Luftwaffe was sending over. One great success for the squadron came when it was providing withdrawal cover for a force of B.17's at 28,000 feet and managed to destroy four FW 190s and damage another.

For 85 and their new companions 96, operations continued immediately after the Christmas festivities as the Luftwaffe lull came to an end. The new Mark X radar now fitted to nearly all the Mosquitoes of 85 was on trial as the first of the New Year confrontations took place. Again the team of Cunningham and Rawnsley found success and on 21 January the Luftwaffe put on the heaviest raid since the winter of 1940-1 with nearly 200 aircraft. FW 190s and ME 410s first came in and dropped 'window' — strips of tinfoil designed to confuse our GCI stations — followed by JU 88s and DO 217s to inflict damage. It was 'B' flight of 85 who were on standby patrol that night and in the ensuing battle they shot down three and damaged a fourth out of the total of sixteen shot down over the British Isles that night. At the end of the night's operations, 85 had reached the magic number of 200 kills by day and night. For John Cunningham and his navigator Jimmie Rawnsley, it was their 20th victim and with rumours of Cunningham's departure to Group Headquarters, it was a fitting last success. With this number reached by 85, West Malling personnel subscribed to present a piece of plate to the squadron in recognition of their achievements. It was suitably inscribed and presented to John Cunningham for 85 Squadron at a huge party held in their honour.

For West Malling it was also a time to take stock as the airfield's own tally at this time reached 26 victories by day, 93 by night with 12 and 13 probables and 22 and 27 damaged. Wing Commander J. A. O'Neill DFC took over command of the station from Wing Commander T. N. Hayes on 1st February and the station strength remained at 85 and 96 Squadrons flying by night and 124 by day.

Towards the end of February the Luftwaffe sent several fighter/bombers over on a retaliatory attack on Kent airfields, something that they had not done since 1943. Four or five 190s flew in the vicinity of the airfield and dropped their bombs. None actually landed on the station, but several chicken houses within the boundary of the airfield suffered casualties, much to the anguish of the farmer. In compensation, 96 saw to it that only two of the raiders reached home.

As February ran into March, the 100th night success was achieved by Flight Lieutenant N. S. Head of 85. To mark the occasion, a performance of Noel Coward's *Private Lives* was performed in the station theatre by Kay Hammond, John Clements and a first class support company. The month also saw every Mosquito of 85 and 96 equipped with the new A1 radar and both squadrons gained further success as John Cunningham left his beloved 85. He was succeeded by Wing Commander C. M. Miller, but not before he had been sent on his way in the customary manner.

It was about this time that the words 'D-Day' were first spoken behind closed doors. For some time now the idea of an Allied offensive into Europe had been tossed about and by March 1944 it was well established as it brought about a new phase of operations for West Malling.

On the 18th of the month, 124 took their Spitfires to Church Fenton and in the afternoon of the same day, 616 returned to their former airfield now equipped with Spitfire VII's and XIV's and commanded by Squadron Leader L. W. Watts DFC. In April they were joined by 91 flying Spitfire XII's and XIV's and both squadrons were now attached to the 2nd Tactical Air Force in preparation for the 'D-Day' landings.

With night fighters and day fighters once again side by side at West Malling, the station entered a new era of operations. At the end of March rumours began to circulate concerning 85 Squadron. They had flown from Malling for nearly a year and though the rumours came as a surprise to many personnel, the shock of reality was a bitter blow. The rumours became fact on 30 April when a signal was received stating that 85 was to join 100 Group of Bomber support aircraft. On 1 May they departed to Swannington, but fate was to ordain that it would not be long before they returned to West Malling.

The night fighting was now left to 96 who ably carried on the good work of shooting down enemy aircraft by night as 91 and 616 of the 2nd Tactical Air Force were to continue flying by day. As a prelude to the Allied landings in France, the Americans made an unopposed landing at Hollandia in Dutch New Guinea (22 April) and the 14th Army began its attack on Assam (5 May). The curtain was beginning to rise on the biggest offensive of the entire war.

As the date for re-entry into Europe came nearer, General Sir Bernard Montgomery, as he then was, flew into West Malling to discuss the coming use of the airfield in support of his troops who would invade the French coast. He made several visits, arriving in his own Miles Messenger which already sported Invasion stripes. Meetings were held in strict security.

Though 85 Squadron had now departed to Swannington, the dispersals and mess accommodation did not remain empty for long. Within two hours of their departure 29 returned to their former home, beating up the field as they arrived. They quickly settled into their old station and one day later were joined by 409 (Canadian) Squadron also equipped with the Mosquito. Squadron Leader Watts of 616 received a signal notifying him that his squadron was to leave for Fairwood Common immediately and by the end of May, with so many changes having taken place over the past few weeks, West Malling was left with 29, 96 and 409 flying Mosquitoes and 91 flying Spitfires.

The date for the invasion was fixed for 5 June 1944 and the operation was deemed to be the beginning of the end of the war for Germany. 91 Squadron with its high flying Spitfires took many valuable photographs of both the Allied landing areas and the enemy's movements. May proved to be a good month for the Malling squadrons and with the summer nights approaching and fair weather expected, an increase in trade came for the night fighters. 29 Squadron, now commanded by Wing Commander P. W. Arbon DFC and flying the Mosquito XIII, ranged far over Northern France, the Low Countries and even Germany itself, attacking communications centres and enemy aircraft on the ground.

Around the perimeter of the airfield quite close to the 'Startled Saint', still a favourite with the squadrons, a single observation tower was being built. Standing about a hundred feet high and giving a good view of approaching aircraft as well as the airfield itself, it was being constructed for the Royal Artillery as a mounting for a 40 mm anti-aircraft gun. It was designed as two independent towers, one to support the gun and the other for a predictor, the upper platform being separated by a one-inch gap to prevent the sensitive prediction instrument being affected by the vibration of gunfire. It was intended that the anti-aircraft/observation tower would be manned by Army personnel and the RAF Regiment for the purpose of airfield defence and to warn the control tower of approaching enemy aircraft. In the event

The unique warning tower built near West Malling for airfield defence. *Author*

it was not finished by the end of the war and therefore served no useful purpose. However, it was, and still is, unique in that no other airfield in the British Isles had a similar tower.

With June fast approaching the day and night attacks into deepest Germany gathered momentum. This increase in bombing also brought maximum danger to aircraft and their crews as one incident at West Malling in late May bore evidence. Some 200 B.17s had taken off from their base in East Anglia to attack the German ball-bearing factory at Schweinfurt. Crossing the French coast they were confronted by a little light flak, but nothing to really worry about. It was as they crossed the German border that it became plain that the enemy was out to devastate this particular raid. Messerschmitt 109s and Focke Wulf 190s seemed to fill the sky as the B.17s began their bombing runs: Many of the aircraft were shot down before releasing their bombs and many more were so badly shot up that they jettisoned their loads and turned for home.

At West Malling it was not uncommon to see a wide variety of aircraft, both British and American, sitting on the grass in front of the control tower. Being one of the nearest airfields to the exit and entry points for bombers over the south coast, it was obvious that it was a haven for aircraft in trouble. After the raid on Schweinfurt, it was West Malling that one of the American crews made for.

At about 3.30 p.m. one of them barely crossed the coast and losing height made for West Malling. Minutes later the aircraft was in the vicinity of the airfield and with his radio out of action, the pilot flew low over the field indicating that he was in trouble. In the aircraft the order was given to jettison anything of weight to lessen the load before attempting a crash landing. Armament, machine guns and survival equipment were all thrown out within the area of West Malling. With the B.17 managing to climb to about 1,000 feet, orders were then given to the crew to bale out. This they did, many of them landing in the villages around the airfield. The pilot continued to fly around the area in an attempt to lose the fuel that he still had on board. Encompassing the villages of Aylesford and Hunton, he flew in a circle for about thirty-five minutes whilst the emergency services at the airfield prepared for his landing. At approximately 4.10 p.m., the B.17 turned on short finals and lined up for the grass runway. Throttling right back and crossing the threshold very low, the pilot dropped it onto the grass successfully and with the emergency services keeping pace with it, the aircraft slewed safely to a halt.

In the many villages surrounding the airfield, instructions in emergency wartime regulations meant that it was the job of the local police to collect all parachutists seen to drop. The job was allocated to two special constables who spent the rest of the afternoon and early evening collecting the American airmen.

When the crew enquired as to the fate of their aircraft, they were amazed to learn that the pilot had got it down in one piece. It made the day complete for two of the crew who had landed near the large house of a local brewer at Hunton and, naturally, the local hospitality had taken over. By the time the police reached them they were in no condition to travel back to Malling. Free whisky and the attention of several lovely ladies had taken their toll! For this particular aircraft and crew it was a happy ending, but for many it was quite the reverse.

On 3 June 1944 Hitler authorised Kesselring to withdraw from Rome and the next day the 5th Army marched into the city. With foul weather prevailing, General Eisenhower postponed the invasion of France for twenty-four hours and the crews of the West Malling squadrons, ready geared for the operation, stood down. With a promise of a slight improvement for 6th June, the General decided that the risk must be taken and that D-Day had to be on that day.

At 02.00 hours on the morning of the 6th with the Channel somewhat less than calm, the first of twelve convoys moved into position and the assault was on. History has documented the invasion repeatedly and at its

A Spitfire of 322 Squadron with Dutch aircrew. *IWM*

conclusion it was deemed a great success, though with a terrifying loss of life. By 08.00 hours on the morning of the 6th, Allied aircraft had flown 7,500 sorties, both bombers and fighters maintaining close support for the troops below and endeavouring to keep the skies overhead free from enemy aircraft.

At West Malling all four squadrons took part in the offensive, the Mosquitoes of 29, 96 and 409 and the Spitfires of 91 being a welcome tonic to the troops battling far below. By the next day the Allies had established a good foothold in France and for the four squadrons it was back to normal operations. Normal that is for six days, for at this time the enemy was about to unleash a formidable weapon upon the British people. At the same time a new type of twin-engined aircraft arrived at West Malling for a fleeting visit. It was a Gloster Meteor, the first jet aircraft to be in service with the RAF and now equipping 616 (South Yorkshire) Squadron, one of the former residents at the station. Somehow flying would never be the same!

The night of Monday, 12 June 1944, passed quietly for the county of Kent. Not much enemy activity was reported by the sector controllers in No. 11 Group at Bentley Priory, Stanmore in Middlesex. At 00.40 in the early morning of 13th June, Folkestone reported that it was being heavily shelled by the long-range German guns along the Pas de Calais in France. One hour later, Maidstone, just a short distance from the airfield, also reported heavy shelling. At 04.09 the duty crew at Bentley Priory were thinking of bed and a well-earned sleep as they sat around the control table waiting for some enemy action. For one of the WAAF operators it was enough that she had heard little action on this particular shift until at 04.10 she heard the words 'Diver – Diver' through her headset. She repeated the code-words aloud and immediately the entire operations room forgot their fatigue and stared in amazement as an extraordinary track progressed across the table at great speed heading towards London.

The coastal radar stations had reported nothing approaching on their screens, nothing that is to distinguish a very low-flying object from the normal traffic and blips on the cathode tubes. The words 'Diver – Diver' had been said by two Royal Observer Corps members perched on a Martello Tower at Dymchurch on Romney Marsh. The post was known as Mike 2 and was one of the early warning posts in the event that the radar chain became inoperable. The two Observers plotted the low-flying craft heading towards Pluckley whose post in turn plotted it to the Lenham zone. Leaving their area, it was handed over to No. 19 Group Headquarters at Bromley when suddenly in between Dartford and Gravesend, the object with the fiery tail stopped emitting flame from the back and the nose tipped downwards. It dived to earth and crashed with a terrific explosion on waste ground at Swanscombe. The time was 04.20 hours and the first Flying Bomb, or V1, had crashed on British soil.

Before it had crashed at Swanscombe, the same two Observers who initially saw it were plotting another as it flew over Dymchurch. This V1 continued inland and crashed at Crouch near Borough Green, no distance from the airfield. A third crossed the coast minutes later and crashed at Cuckfield in Sussex. With the aiming point being the Tower of London, the Vergeltungs 1 or Retaliation 1 weapon was about to begin its reign of terror.

With this new and destructive type of warfare, West Malling became the main base for coping with the menace and this in turn ensured that the airfield was given over to the day fighters. The night fighter squadrons began to move out with 29 and 409 leaving on 19 June and 96 following on the 20th. Since 1942 West Malling had become known as the premier night fighter base in Fighter Command, but now it was to be the turn of the day fighters to combat the V1s. On the first day of the assault ten V1s were launched with five reaching the Kent coast. There was then a two-day pause and the next phase was when two hundred and forty-four were launched against London. West Malling prepared itself for the onslaught.

With 91 Squadron already at the airfield they were joined on 20th June by 322 flying the Spitfire XIV. Together the squadrons devised methods of

The menace leaves its launch pad in the Pas de Calais in June 1944. *R. Humphreys*

It flies over Kent. *IWM*

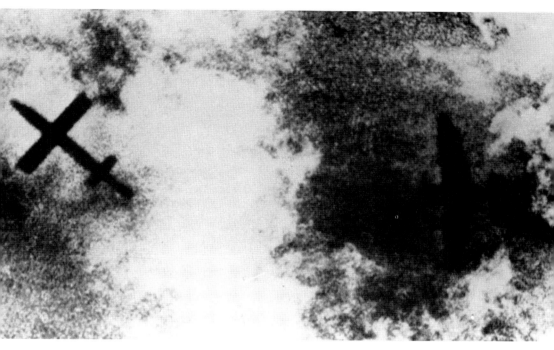

A Spitfire closes on its prey. *IWM*

And brings its wings up under the wings of the V1. *IWM*

The wreckage of a V1 lies in an orchard at Horsmonden near West Malling. One of the squadrons operating from the base shot it down. Kent Messenger

bringing the robots down before they reached their target. The obvious way was to shoot them down, but this could only be accomplished by the attacking aircraft remaining some distance away from the V1 for fear of the explosion damaging or destroying it, the distance not being conducive to firing a true burst of gunfire.

The other method used was equally dangerous and was discovered by Roland Beamont, later to become a famous test pilot, while flying a Hawker Tempest on a V1 attack. Formatting alongside he gradually brought his wing up to within six inches of the V1's own wing. Holding this position for some time, the airflow over both wings took effect and the rocket dipped and keeled over to its death. In the end this method became standard for the West Malling squadrons.

Slowly the toll of rockets brought down gathered momentum. In June alone as launchings from France increased, 91 Squadron had a credit of 184 V1's and 322 by July had claimed 108 destroyed. Fitted with the powerful Griffon engine, the XI V mark of Spitfire was the ideal fighter for this work and the best individual achievement was by Flying Officer Brugwal of 322 Squadron who on 8 July managed to claim five rockets.

During June many of the V1's fell close to the airfield and towards the end of the month it seemed as though Kent was littered with metal from these robots. Flaming June gave way to a warm July and on the 5th of the month,

157 Squadron flew the Mosquito NF 30 from the base in 1944.

with the launchings of V1's increasing daily, two more squadrons joined 91 and 322 at West Malling. No. 80 flying the Spitfire IX flew in from Gatwick, and the same day 274 arrived with their IX's, although they were shortly to convert to the Hawker Tempest. West Malling with four squadrons was once again a frontline airfield. With constant readiness from dawn to dusk the squadrons put in a very full day, sometimes being scrambled eight or nine times, but for the local people it guaranteed a full night's sleep with no night fighters to bother them, something for which they were indeed grateful!

July was hot as the battle continued, but for the Germans the entire war campaign was falling apart. Hitler, on the 20th was, himself, the target of a bomb plot which failed and all over the world the Allies were proving victorious. The V1 campaign, however, seemed to be gathering momentum as in July the enemy threw even greater efforts into this last major operation. On the 21st 91 and 322 Squadrons left West Malling and were replaced by 157 flying the Mosquito XIX whilst 85 returned for a further period at the base. Both these squadrons had been pulled from No. 100 Group to help combat the V1's and, with their arrival, the airfield became the foremost anti-diver airfield in Fighter Command.

157 made themselves at home and the officers requisitioned the lovely Addington House at Addington for their mess. During an off-duty period for 157 some of the personnel discovered that a roadhouse on the Tonbridge to

How West Malling looked before closure in 1944. *RAF Museum*

Sevenoaks road named the 'Hilden Manor' had a luxurious swimming pool within its grounds. It was immediately recruited for dinghy drill practice, the crews then retiring to the hostelry itself. For 85 it was back to the Manor House, their favourite haunt. They found the Twitch Inn virtually as they had left it and took no time at all hanging a notice by the door which read: 'open all hours'.

By 31 July West Malling could claim 278 V1s destroyed. The rapid turnaround in squadrons was an indication of the strain that this type of operation had upon the majority of the crews, the average length of stay for diver operations varying from one to two months.

In August 274 Squadron converted to the Tempest and on the 4th of the month 316 (City of Warsaw) Polish Squadron arrived from Coltishall. For the first time in its history, West Malling was parent to an American fighter for 316 were equipped with the North American Mustang III, a very potent aircraft powered by a Packard Merlin engine. They had been taken off the strength of the 2nd Tactical Air Force in order to rejoin Fighter Command in its fight against the V1.

The newly erected Officers' Mess in 1946.

In August the V1 launchings increased to between 250 and 300 a day. All the squadrons were in daily contact with the robots, resulting in less than half reaching London. 17th August saw 316 Squadron leave the base and on the 28th, 157 departed having done their tour on anti-diver operations. One day later 85 left again for Swannington and 100 Group and 80 moved to Manston in Kent in partnership with 274. The reason for the sudden departure of the squadrons from West Malling became obvious as the end of August approached and the daily launchings of the V1s declined dramatically. The Allies with their fast progress across Europe had overrun the rocket launching sites and, although the offensive was continued on a limited scale by V1s launched from German aircraft over the North Sea, the campaign was petering-out. In all over 8,500 rockets were launched against the United Kingdom, barely 2,500 got through to their target. For the Royal Air Force at West Malling, the anti-diver operations had been a great success and the total tally for the airfield was over 280 V1s destroyed.

By 31 August 1944 the base was abandoned, but it was already being earmarked as a major base in peacetime. Tremendous extensions and a new concrete runway would be needed for the post-war RAF and jet aircraft and although the closure of West Malling seemed premature, for war was to rage another year, from April 1941 until August 1944, the station claimed to have been responsible for the destruction of 165 enemy aircraft, together with 34 probably destroyed, 59 damaged and 280 V1s destroyed. It was quite an achievement and peacetime was to see the airfield again become the premier night fighter base of the RAF.

CHAPTER 7

THE UNEASY PEACE THAT PREVAILED

When it closed prematurely in 1944, West Malling was still a grass airfield and with the battle of the V1 firmly behind it, the Air Ministry decided that with the expected uneasy peace that generally followed a war, the airfield would be expanded to accommodate two regular and one auxiliary squadrons. During its closure the RAF appointed Squadron Leader G. T. Block as Commanding Officer and he in turn handed over to Squadron Leader H. Baxter MM on 9 March 1945.

The main job of reconstruction fell to 5011 Squadron who supervised local contractors. Work took until June 1945. At the end of that month, West Malling was again declared operational, the first task of the base being to act as a rehabilitation centre for returning Prisoners of War.

As the big transport aircraft landed on the newly laid runway 07/25 the documentation and kitting out of ex-PoW's began in the new station headquarters and administration offices. Many of the prisoners were bewildered and for the majority West Malling was the first place of sanity they had seen in many years. Repatriation continued for some months and it was not until 10 September that an operational squadron became resident at the base.

With the final intake of prisoners leaving, 287 Squadron flew in from Bradwell Bay to re-open the station. Flying the very fast Spitfire XVI, their task was to work in co-operation with local ack-ack and naval units. This involved a certain amount of target towing, the evidence of which was sometimes to be seen entangled in trees around the airfield perimeter. A week later No. 1003 Servicing Wing arrived to take on the task of squadron servicing.

As part of the Victory celebrations that were to take place nationwide, it was decided that West Malling would participate, to show the people of Kent just how a peacetime fighter airfield would operate. Mustangs, Spitfires, Tempests and Mosquitoes together with a new Meteor jet fighter

The control tower at West Malling. This was built in 1942 and was in use until the closure of the airfield.

29 Squadron return in 1946 with Mosquito NF 30s. Pictured are Wing Commander Allan DFC, DSO with two of his pilots. *Kent Messenger*

On 8 June 1946 the Victory flypast took place over the Capital. One of the squadrons using West Malling was 247 with Vampire F1 and 3s, one of which is shown here. *P. Edmunds*

gave a most impressive display and flypast to a large audience assembled at the airfield, the entire show culminating in a flypast over Maidstone. A final reminder of the past years of war was on 1 October 1945 when a Liberator landed following earlier wartime internment in Switzerland. As it taxied to a stop beside the restructured control tower, the crew were met by many high-ranking officials from the Air Ministry who had flown into West Malling especially for the occasion and to witness the last operation of the war.

287 was the sole resident at the airfield until 29 October when 29 Squadron again brought their Mosquito NF 30s from Manston to West Malling as part of the post-war fighter defence force. With Wing Commander J. W. Allan DSO, DFC leading the squadron, the aircraft and aircrew were settled in by nightfall leaving the rest of the personnel to arrive by car and train that evening or the next morning. The new dispersal areas and hangars were a welcome sight for 29 as they well-remembered the situation back in 1942. This was indeed luxury to them and yet somehow, in the aftermath of war, it was difficult to settle into a routine for peacetime service, and for some months many wartime tactics were still used in the new training programme. While this caused no real problems with the Mosquitoes, the impending change-over to jet aircraft meant that new style tactics would have to be learnt and practised.

For the remaining months of 1945, 287 and 29 Squadrons worked in close co-operation. The officers were still using the Manor House, but with the construction of a new mess on the airfield site the Manor House was officially de-requisitioned on 10 January 1946. This was a sad day for many as it passed from the care of the night fighter squadrons who had used it for so many years and was returned intact to its former owners.

500 Squadron and their Mosquitoes in 1946. The Commanding Officer is Squadron Leader Pat Green. *R. Moss*

29 Squadron takes the Royal Salute in October 1945. *W. O. Lewis*

The AOC inspects 29 Squadron's Mosquitos. *Mr Wells via D. Collyer*

Many lectures were taking place at this time with the transition from a war to a peacetime RAF. For 29 it seemed as though they were becoming very deskbound, but with air-to-air firing exercises and interception practice life once again became very pleasant at West Malling. On 1 February 1946 fourteen aircraft and crews left for a spell of firing practice at Spilsby, a very isolated gunnery range on the coast. The Operations Record Book records that the accommodation was sparse after the luxury of Malling, canvas quarters being no substitute for brick.

The first six months of the year were to bring the same routine of lectures and flying. In May, 29 Squadron flew six aircraft in a flypast over the Channel Islands for the victory celebrations and in June it had the honour of leading a Mosquito flypast over London. Though the weather was abysmal, many thousands of people were seen to be lining the streets of the capital.

It was now time for 287 Squadron to be disbanded. They had been formed primarily for the task of providing target towing facilities for the RAF and with the peacetime operations now applying, no longer was this expensive operation needed. At a ceremony at West Malling, the colours of the squadron were laid to rest in the station chapel on 15 June 1946.

In August three aircraft were detached to Tangmere in Sussex for High Speed Flight trials and at the same time it was announced that West Malling was to receive another regular squadron and an auxiliary. For a year 29 had been the only night fighter squadron and now they were to be joined by 25 and the County of Kent Auxiliary Squadron 500.

It was the auxiliaries who arrived first, forming on 10 May after stand-down at the end of the war. 500 had undertaken sterling service both in the UK and abroad during the conflict and in their wisdom, the Air Ministry had decided to reform all auxiliary units as soon as possible after the end of the war. The Commanding Officer, Squadron Leader Patrick Green OBE, AFC, immediately began an intensive recruitment campaign throughout the county and within two months the squadron was up to full strength allowing the allocated number of Mosquito NF 30s to fly into West Malling.

A spirit of camaraderie quickly developed between the regulars and the auxiliaries and this was further strengthened on 6 September 1946 when 25 Squadron brought their Mosquito NF 36s to the base making it once again the front-line night fighter station in the defence of the United Kingdom.

Wing Commander Ingle, the Commanding Officer of West Malling, was on the newly-laid tarmac to welcome 25 as they flew in from Boxted. Once the aircraft had settled into their dispersals and the men had been allocated messing accommodation he addressed the personnel of both squadrons, stating that they were to work in close liaison with each other to help maintain the uneasy peace in the world.

From 1946 to 1950, the standard RAF night fighter was the Mosquito NF 30 or 36, equipped with A1 Mk. 10 radar, similar to the mark used during

25 Squadron bring their Mosquito NF 36s for peacetime operations. *J. Rawlings*

The Air Officer Commanding No. 11 Group inspects 25 Squadron in 1947. The Station Commander, Wing Commander Pedley, is fourth from the left. *T. Moor*

the latter stages of the war. The RAF did not expect the night version of the Meteor jet fighter until well into the 1950s and with recent world events, it was plain to see that the service required a stop gap jet to replace the ageing Mosquitoes. Whilst the political wranglings were taking place, it was announced that West Malling was to receive a third regular squadron and on 16 April 1947, 85 returned once more to their former home and favourite airfield. Arriving from Tangmere the Mosquitoes swept in low over the field before turning and landing on runway 25.

Meanwhile the County of Kent Auxiliary Squadron had been carrying out their weekend duties flying the Mosquito NF 30, but during 1947 it was announced that forthwith, all auxiliary squadrons would be converted to a daytime fighter role. The NF 30s were flown to a maintenance unit in Wales and on 6 October 1948, 500 received the new Meteor F Mk. 3 fighter, the first auxiliary squadron to do so. Conversion to the type progressed so well that Squadron Leader Kennard, now the CO of 500, was able to take the

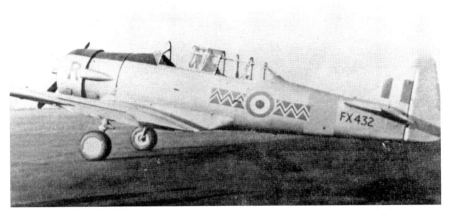

Flying Training for 500 Squadron was carried out on the Harvard. *Airfix*

squadron to annual camp at Thorney Island in Hampshire. The honorary Air Commodore of the squadron, Sir Anthony Eden, paid a visit and was shown the intricacies of the Meteor 3. Taking a great interest, he started the engines of the aircraft and later announced that it was an incredible experience to be with a squadron now flying such an aircraft.

The three night fighter squadrons at West Malling were still flying the Mosquito NF 36 in the night defence role. It had been rumoured for some time that all three squadrons were to go jet powered, but it fell to 25 to inaugurate the jet night fighter. It was decided that they would convert to the De Havilland NF 10 Vampire, but prior to receiving the type the squadron had three Vampire FB 5s delivered for pilot training on 23 January 1951. By July they had received the Vampire NF 10s and conversion from the Mosquito was relatively easy due to a similar cockpit layout. Apparently the only grouse came from the Armourers because of the difficult access to the guns in the belly, a lot of brawn and endless patience being needed. Never a really successful aircraft because of its single engine and lack of ejector seats, the RAF received them as a stop-gap between the Mosquitoes and the Meteor night fighters. 25, however, worked them up to a good operational standard and for the squadron it was to prove a most enjoyable flying machine. Its safety record was very good and the only really bad incident with it took place on 12 June 1952 involving 25 Squadron. In bad conditions one morning, a Vampire of the squadron was on finals into the airfield when it collided with a Royal Naval Oxford that was just leaving the West Malling circuit. The Oxford crashed at Maidstone killing both the crew whilst the Vampire managed a forced landing back at West Malling.

Sixth and last version of the Mosquito was the NF 36 seen here in the colours of 85 Squadron. Aircraft is RL 148. *J. Rawlings*

Instruction for Air Cadets was carried out by 500 Squadron. *R. Moss*

In May 1949, 500 went jet powered, the first auxiliary squadron to do so, and converted to the Gloster Meteor Mk. 3. *G. Cardew*

500 at annual camp at Thorney Island with their Honorary Air Commodore Anthony Eden. *Hampshire Telegraph*

The weekend airmen get to know the new aircraft. *Kent Messenger*

500 refuelling a Meteor. *MOD*

During the early 1950s, two extra T-Type hangars were constructed to house the jet aircraft that were coming into service.

The subsequent investigation found airfield control at fault and no blame was to be attached to the aircraft type. When the NF 10s were exchanged for Meteors in 1954, 25 Squadron had lost only three which, in comparison with other types in service, was a good record.

For 85 it was direct conversion to the Meteor NF 11 on 4 September 1951. There appeared to be no rivalry between the two jet squadrons as they trained side by side. Not so for 29 who were not to go jet-powered at West Malling. They departed to Tangmere on 30 November 1950 and converted to the Meteor a year later. The fighting force at West Malling was now 25 and 85 plus 500, the auxiliaries.

Group Captain H. N. G. Ramsbottom Isherwood DFC, AFC relinquished his command of the airfield to Group Captain H. S. Darley DSO on 12 June 1950 and it was this Commanding Officer who brought West Malling onto a war footing when the Korean crisis erupted. 98 Squadron, who had been at West Malling on detachment with Mosquito bombers, left as the repercussions at the airfield became far reaching. 500, the auxiliary squadron, was put onto a permanent status for three to six months. Civilian occupations were held open as the territorial or part time airmen reported for regular duty. The squadron had just replaced their Mk. 3 Meteors with the Mk. 4 and were in the process of working them up to operational status when the call came for active service. 500 was detached to Tangmere for

25 was the first regular squadron to go jet powered at the base. The Vampire NF 10s are pictured on the hardstanding. *J. Rawlings*

A fine shot of WP 242 prior to start-up. *PRO*

The presentation of the standard to 25 Squadron on 25 June 1954. By then the squadron had converted to Meteors. *PRO*

The CO of 500 had his own tailplane painted on his Mk. 8 to symbolise the County of Kent. The main part was blue to represent the blue sky and the pattern was white to represent the white cliffs of Dover, and green to represent the green fields of Kent. *G. Cardew*

25 Squadron with NF 10s taxi past the tower. *25 Squadron*

Many squadrons were detached to West Malling for the Coronation Review of the RAF. Pictured in the foreground are NF 12s of 141 Squadron. *D. Buchanan*

the last three weeks of the crisis period and when it became obvious that the situation was not as bad as had originally been envisaged, it returned to West Malling and stood down, continuing its auxiliary duties.

The regular squadrons at West Malling had been put on full readiness from the beginning of the Korean conflict and had taken on a wartime role. Aircraft were armed and fuelled ready at the dispersals and the crews were attending many lectures and briefing sessions behind closed doors. When the situation became calmer, they, like the auxiliaries, returned to normal peacetime duties.

Throughout 1952 and 53 the squadrons remained unchanged at the airfield. One exception was the Commanding Officer, Group Captain Darley who left on 18 July 1952 and was succeeded by Group Captain E. W. Whitley DSO, DFC. He was replaced in September by Group Captain P. R. Walker and that same month the annual RAF at Home Battle of Britain displays began with West Malling taking a prominent part. By early morning on 15 September, the airfield was crowded with thousands of people, all anxious to see just what they were getting for their taxes. They were not disappointed as 25, 85 and 500 put on many superb flying displays.

On 7 August 1953 Group Captain P. H. Hamley AFC took command of West Malling at about the same time as 85 exchanged its Meteor NF 11s for the newer Mk. 12. Shortly after, 500 received the Mk. 8 Meteor and one year later, 25 converted to the Meteor 12 from the Vampires.

A new squadron arrived at the airfield on 28 February 1955 in the shape of 153 Squadron, also equipped with Meteor 12 and 14s. Together with 25 and 85, they worked up to an operational standard and again all three regular squadrons gave flying displays at the Battle of Britain displays held that year.

With the arrival of 153, West Malling became an all Meteor airfield and this was to continue until 1955 when 153 departed for Waterbeach in Cambridgeshire. Not much information is available for this period regarding the operations of the regular squadrons at the airfield due to the records still being held under a secret classification. Not so, however, for the auxiliaries who in 1953 flew their Meteor F 8s to Takali in Malta for summer camp. It did of course prove to be a very popular camp with 100 per cent attendance and a very bronzed squadron returned to base two weeks later. Squadron Leader D. M. Clause AFC assumed command in 1954 and again the squadron went to Malta for camp. This was also the year that the squadron won the coveted 'Cooper' trophy, an annual award given to the most efficient auxiliary squadron. Another triumph for 500 was the award in 1956 of the 'Esher' trophy and the receiving of the Freedom of the Borough of Maidstone. A parade and march-past was highlighted only by the over flight of the squadron Meteors just above the Town Hall.

The Mk. 8s of 500 were all named after Kentish cities or towns. Pictured is City of Canterbury. *G. Cardew*

An NF 12 of 153 taken at a Battle of Britain display at West Malling.

Flying Officers O'Donovan and Allison of 85 get airborne in 1955. *85 Squadron*

500 fly over Kent. *Gloster Aircraft*

The Esher Trophy awarded to 500 Squadron is marched into the ranks for the last time on 16 February 1957. *Photo Section RAF West Malling*

This was followed by a march through Maidstone. *Photo Section RAF West Malling*

Above: The disbandment parade of 500. *Kent Messenger*

Right: Flying Officers L. Fitch and M. Vaughan of 85 in their NF 14. *85 Squadron*

A Meteor 8 of the station flight in camouflage, *c.* 1958.

85 Squadron NF 14 over Yalding in 1956. *A. S. Thomas*

It was with heavy hearts that the news of the disbandment of the Auxiliary Air Force squadrons reached 500 early in 1957. Neither the Battle Honours claimed nor the trophies won could change the minds of the Defence Ministry and with the 'stand-down' official, the 'Esher' trophy was paraded for the last time on 16 February 1957. March saw the official discharge of the Auxiliary Air Force and, in common with all the other units, 500 were stood-down. It was a sad day at West Malling for the regular squadrons to witness the final parade of the squadron for they had come to regard their part-time colleagues as a fine unit. Little did 25 and 85 Squadrons realise that their time of departure from West Malling was also fast approaching.

Above: A fine shot of 85 Squadron Meteors NF 11s preparing for a day's flying.
Below: The last days of West Malling in 1989. *L. Pilkington*

CHAPTER 8

THE END IS IN SIGHT

With the departure of 500 Squadron, West Malling was left with 25 and 85 both now flying Meteor 12 and 14s. This union did not, however, last long for 25 took their aircraft to Tangmere on 30 September 1957 and 85 took theirs to Church Fenton on 23 September. For an airfield that had contributed so much to keep the peace, it was sad to see it abandoned once again. It was not to remain so for long as the construction gangs moved in once more and commenced a building programme to bring the airfield up to standard for the new generation of jet fighters for the 1960s. It took just over a year and on 5 August 1959, 85 returned once more, now equipped with the Gloster Javelin FAW 2. This was the first twin-jet Delta fighter in the world and was designed to have a very high performance with long endurance. It was a very noisy aircraft and for sometime after its arrival the complaints came flooding in to the Commanding Officer of West Malling, now Wing Commander F. N. Brinsden. The Mk. 6 was received in late 1959 and again, not much can be said about this period of operations at the airfield due to the 30-year rule regarding secrets still being in force. Suffice to say the squadron contributed to the peace of the time and with Mk. 8 Javelins arriving in early 1960, it seemed as though continuing operations at West Malling were assured.

On 4 August 1959 Group Captain C. Foxley-Norris DSO arrived to command the base. The javelins were a constant source of complaint for the local residents, one local farmer even complaining that the noisy aircraft put his chickens off laying. He presented a bill for lost revenue to the policeman on duty at the main guardroom who tactfully took the bill assuring the farmer that his complaint would be noted.

In July 1960 Wing Commander F. N. Brinsden came back as Commanding Officer of West Malling. This was at a time when rumours were being whispered that in the next round of defence cuts, the RAF would be ordered to reduce its bases in the United Kingdom. The review duly came and it was

The Gloster Javelin arrives. Pictured is a FAW 2 of 85 Squadron in 1960.

A Mk. 8 undergoes maintenance in the hangar. *MOD*

announced that several flying bases, including West Malling, were indeed to close. On 8 September 1960 85 Squadron left for West Raynham in Norfolk and, although more construction had recently been done at West Malling, it did not secure it from closure and six months later the airfield was placed on a care and maintenance basis.

West Malling took on a very forlorn look as the station personnel began to close the station down. The weeds began to grow on the hard standings and runway almost immediately and the crew rooms nestling under the protection of the hangars began to deteriorate. The New Year of 1961 saw no future use for the airfield as an operational station within Fighter Command. It was stated that the new enemy now faced us on the East Coast and therefore the majority of defence airfields would be situated along that side of the country. It was further added that West Malling lay dangerously within the corridors of the civil airlines who passed overhead on their way to Gatwick at no great height. The Spitfire that had been placed at the entrance to honour all those who had flown from the airfield was removed and transported to Leuchars in Scotland. By late 1961 the station had formally stood-down, the RAF flag was no longer flying from its pole outside Station Headquarters and a private security company had taken over as guardians of the airfield.

It seemed as though the airfield was forgotten as the trees and weeds were allowed to grow unmolested. From April 1941 until its premature closure

The Yanks arrive! The Super R4D (Dakota) nicknamed 'The Admiral's Barge' in 1962. *US Navy*

in August 1944, West Malling had claimed to have been responsible for the destruction of 165 enemy aircraft together with 34 probably destroyed and 59 damaged. It was some record of achievement.

It was, however, not entirely forgotten as in 1962 West Malling entered yet another stage and, although the new residents spoke English, it was spoken in a very drawling manner for the Yanks had arrived in force.

It was about this period that the United States Forces were expanding within the NATO framework and were basing many units in the United Kingdom. One of them was a Naval Facility Flight based at Hendon in Middlesex, this airfield itself also under threat of closure. The United States authorities looked for another airfield not too far from Hendon and when knowledge of West Malling came their way they approached the Ministry of Defence, as it was by then known. The Ministry sanctioned the proposals and almost immediately the withdrawal from Hendon began. The 'Yanks' had arrived.

The Naval Facility was the Fleet Air Support Squadron 200, the purpose of which was to support US Naval units in Western Europe. The aircraft that they flew comprised a Convair R4Y (Convair 340) named 'Samaritan' and known as the 'Admiral's Barge'. It was so named because this particular aircraft was the personal mount of the Commander-in-Chief US Navy Europe, rather like our own Queen's Flight. For general freight and communications duties the Facility had the faithful R4D Super Dakotas, which were the work horses of the squadron, and several SNB 5 Expeditors (Beech 18s) for trainee and refresher flying, mostly by chairborne staff from London. It also had Grumman Albatross Amphibians on the inventory for services with the US Naval Attaché in the Scandinavian area. Regular weekly flights into West Malling were carried out by C.130 Hercules from the American Support Squadron VR 24 based at La Rota in Spain. This was in order to bring in Mediterranean freight and passengers and to carry the regular US mail run. The Facility also had many visiting aircraft from exercising squadrons, mainly anti-submarine P2V Neptunes and P3A Orions plus many carrier-borne aircraft from US aircraft carriers visiting British Naval bases. All of this for an airfield that had recently closed!

The arrival of the Americans received a mixed reception in the town of West Malling. Some, mostly local traders, welcomed them with open arms since their business had declined with the departure of the RAF. Others, notably the local residents and large house owners, were warning each other to lock up their daughters! In the event the Americans rarely left the airfield as they changed the somewhat staid existence of RAF West Malling into a miniature Las Vegas. Some of the billets and messes were changed overnight

Airborne Early Warning Super Constellation at a Navy Open Day. *US Navy*

The weekly Hercules arrives from Spain. *US Navy*

into clubs and 'soda fountains' and the local musicians benefited with a dance nearly every night at the base.

The Naval Facility soon settled in and further cemented relations with the local community when they held a series of open days at the airfield. Many aircraft from other United States bases in Britain arrived to give the Open Days a truly all-American flavour and once again West Malling reverted to its former glory.

The Americans used the base for nearly two years, but again, no records are available of the type of operations that they carried out from West Malling. When Blackbushe aerodrome became available in 1963 it was decided by the US Navy to install the Facility Flights there in preference to an airfield in the centre of Kent. By late 1963 the Americans had left and by the end of the year, West Malling was once again deserted.

The care and maintenance unit returned and whilst the fate of the airfield was again being decided, 618 Volunteer Gliding School arrived from Manston to take up residence and instruct Air Cadets in gliding proficiency. It was now silent flight as the Sedbergh and Slingsby gliders were winched into the air for circuit flying around the airfield. The Gliding School took over part of the RAF dispersal huts to use as their administrative block and one of the T-Type hangars was used for the storage of their aircraft.

Prelude to closure. The main entrance in 1964. *KAHRS*

Decay sets in. The trees begin to grow beside the wartime Blister hangars. *Author*

The gliding school was the sole occupant until 1964 when Short Brothers, the aircraft manufacturing company, decided to bring a servicing flight into West Malling from Rochester where they had been based for a number of years. They moved to the airfield with two Sea Princes, WF 132 and WP 312 and a Varsity WL 681. These aircraft were operated by Shorts on a service contract and Ministry research work and in addition the company also serviced several Chipmunk aircraft used by the Air Experience Flights in the South East. Short Brothers occupied the larger of the four hangars and re-opened the control tower, which had remained closed since the Americans had left. The airfield began to see a few movements though nothing to the scale to which it was accustomed. The servicing unit used the airfield for a number of years, but with the gradual scaling-down of the RAF about this period, Shorts eventually lost the service contract in 1978 and West Malling was once again left with gliders only.

In 1970 the Kent County Council bought the airfield from the Ministry of Defence for £475,000 to protect it from undesirable development. It had long been rumoured that the site was to be sold off to industry or even a hotel chain, but in their future planning the KCC saw its potential as an airfield well into the future. Tonbridge and Malling council moved into the pseudo-Georgian officers' mess that had been built in 1945 and the local and County Council utilised many of the brick buildings for offices and storage facilities. In the mass-exit of British passport holders from Uganda in 1972, West Malling was commissioned as one of the main reception centres for Asians entering Britain. Emergency sleeping accommodation was installed in the former RAF billets for them and many were to remain at West Malling for some considerable time.

Throughout all of this change, 618 Gliding School continued to operate every weekend for the benefit of the Air Cadets and it was about this time that the intentions of the KCC to continue using the airfield for flying became common knowledge. It was not well received in many quarters and almost overnight the local opposition formed itself into an Action Group to try to stop the KCC from carrying out its intention.

Whilst the wranglings were taking place, the RAF returned to West Malling after an absence of sixteen years. It was the famous RAF aerobatic team the Red Arrows who brought their nine Gnats and a Hercules C.130 aircraft to West Malling in 1976 for the purpose of refuelling for an air display being held over the sea front at Ramsgate. The team would normally have used Manston, but this was being re-surfaced at the time and the KCC gave permission for the Ministry to use the airfield. Without any advertising the occasion still attracted over 3,000 people and not one went home disappointed with the afternoon's events.

Meanwhile the local opposition groups were gathering ammunition for a public hearing with regard to further flying at the airfield. Proposals by the KCC for the full exploitation of West Malling with up to 65,000 ATC movements per year by 1990 angered them even further culminating in the proposals being put to the then Environment Secretary Mr Michael Heseltine. After a very heated public enquiry, it was agreed that the airfield could be used for further flying with restrictions, namely, only certain hours being used for movements and severe weight restrictions on the type of aircraft to use the airfield.

CHAPTER 9

THE PRESENT

Meanwhile the KCC, with the approval of the inquiry into further flying from the airfield, began to sound out potential aviation customers. The first moves were made by Television South, the company who had won the franchise from Southern Television to broadcast independent TV programmes in the south. With their main studio in Southampton and a newly built studio in Maidstone, the company used a twin-engined Beechcraft Baron and later an Islander to transport company personnel between the two locations. It chose West Malling as the Maidstone base and operated a two-way service between the airfield and Southampton Airport for a year.

However, it was in 1983 that West Malling really came back into the aviation fold. The KCC leased part of the airfield to an aviation company named Metair Aircraft Equipment Ltd. The company had been in existence for over thirty years, being established in the village of Bexley, Kent, as a subcontractor to the aircraft industry and also a manufacturer of specialised racing and sports cars. The expansion within the aviation business necessitated a move to larger premises at nearby West Street in Erith where major aircraft projects began to be undertaken. A short time later a second factory was established complete with a helicopter landing pad to enable them to take on the extra work connected with aircraft completion. With this expansion the company looked for an airfield within easy reach of Erith. They found West Malling and, when the legal requirements were satisfied, the Civil Aviation Authority amended the airfield classification from a C3 (Civil closed) aerodrome to a C2 (Civil private) aerodrome allowing Metair to move all their operations from Erith to West Malling.

After years of neglect the site had fallen into a sorry state of repair and Metair took upon themselves to rectify much of the damage. They installed runway lighting, high intensity approach lights on runway 07/25, display boards for air traffic control and a full refurbishment of the control tower including the installation of VHF radio and meteorological equipment.

The company began a recruiting campaign aimed at local people with the news that they had been awarded the contract to design, manufacture and install a complete cabin interior and externally finish and paint the new Saab/Fairchild 340 feeder airliners. A twin engine turbo-prop aircraft incorporating all the modern digital cockpit instrumentation of the period, the aircraft was aimed at the inter-city commuter market. The first of many arrived at West Malling during 1984 destined for the Swiss company, Crossair, followed by the first of the type to be exported to the USA and a company named Comair. Further work followed when a contract was issued for the completion of French Puma Helicopters, including the installation of avionics. This again involved upgrading the workforce by which time Metair had been notified that they had become the recipients of a Queen's Award for industry.

It was this resurgence of interest in the airfield that enticed London Weekend Television to choose West Malling as the setting for the American wartime series 'We'll Meet Again'. It also introduced the only airworthy B.17 Flying Fortress in Britain to the airfield. Named 'Sally B' she was representative of the many similar aircraft that flew from bases all over the UK during the Second World War. The series took six months to film and for much of this time Sally B resided at the airfield. She became such a part of the airfield that her operator, Elly Sallingboe and the B.17 Preservation Society decided to hold a vintage air show built around the airfield in 1982. The rest is history as for the next eleven years, the show became the largest and best airshow in the country.

The B.17 G 'Sally B' pictured at West Malling during the filming of *We'll Meet Again* by LWT. *Author*

A Saab 340 of Air Midwest awaits clearance after interior and exterior furbishment by Metair Aircraft Equipment Ltd now resident at the base. *Author*

Cardboard cut-outs of 13.1 Ts create the impression of a busy base during filming. *Author*

At the same time the old Sedbergh and Slingsby gliders of 618 VGS were replaced by German built Vanguard gliders. The school became the envy of other gliding schools when it was announced that each year it attained the highest number of winch launches and wings awarded to cadets than any other. In addition the airfield became well known for parascending and

An aerial shot of the airfield taken in the 1980s. *Kent Messenger*

model aircraft flying yet all of this did not stop the rumblings that Kent County Council were not receiving the amount of revenue that owning the site demanded. They began to explore other avenues including leasing the site to a builder with all the implications that this suggested.

Despite the formation of a group calling themselves 'Save West Malling Group' (SWAG for short) which vigorously campaigned for the retention of the site for flying through several high profile public meetings, the writing was on the wall for West Malling airfield. If confirmation were needed, the news that the county council had leased the airfield to an American company called 'Rouse Ltd' who were prolific in designing and building very large housing estates bought despair to all those who had fought to keep the airfield open. A subsidiary company called 'Rouse (Kent) Ltd' began a series of meetings to show the public their intentions. It became perfectly obvious that the plans did not including any flying and despite so many of the local populace wanting the building plan rejected and the airfield retained as it was, it was all to no avail.

The first casualty was the very fine Air Cadet gliding school, No. 618. Despite looking for another site within Kent, none was found. Eventually the school was re-located to Halton in Buckinghamshire meaning that Kent cadets had to travel a distance for any instruction and flying. It has since moved to Odiham, an operational airfield in Hampshire, which again incurs a lot of travelling. The second unit to receive notice to quit was the superb local employer Metair. Having spent an enormous amount of money on the refurbishment of the airfield, they now had to leave it all behind due to a forced move to Biggin Hill.

The last casualty was the Great Warbirds Airshow who relocated to Wroughton airfield near Swindon after the 1993 show. The event was never the same again and within three years of moving, the best airshow ever ceased to be held.

It was the intention of the Kent County Council to develop the airfield into a high tech business park. The old wartime buildings, full of history, were gradually pulled down leaving just the control tower to remind us of a past history. When the runway was pulled up, the concrete was used as hardcore for the roads and very large industrial units. When it was seen that the take-up for technical premises was not going to reach the intended target, houses became the prime objective, the result of which we see today.

From the air it is difficult to see any outline of an airfield, its identity lost among the thousands of houses already built. This devastation of a truly historic and once beautifully preserved airfield continues today with the media stating that Kingshill (as the airfield site is now known) is the most desirable place to live in the country. For the local populace and people beyond who remember the airfield as it was and who campaigned to keep it open, its desecration was a sad day. The increased traffic that the site generated soon made it obvious that the infrastructure was not capable of handling such a demand, something that had been debated and rejected by the Kent County Council and Rouse (Kent) Ltd. Almost immediately plans were passed to build new roads and spurs from the main M20 Motorway to cope with the problems. Even with this, rush hours are something to be missed if possible.

In June 2000, an off-spring of the 'Save West Malling Group (SWAG)' was formed, intent on making sure that the airfield was never forgotten. Named the 'West Malling Memorial Group' the intention was to place a memorial at the site of the old station headquarters reminding all those who passed of the illustrious history of the site. Designed and built by Mr Gordon Newton of the Stone Shop in East Farleigh near Maidstone, the memorial consists of four polished black granite panels, two metres high and one metre wide. Weighing over one tonne apiece, the first panel features the insignia of the Royal Air Force and that of West Malling airfield. Panels two and three provide information on the operational duties of the station together with interesting anecdotes now 'preserved in stone'. On each of the information panels are pictures of aircraft,

1F22   543/RAF/3514 · 19 AUG 66 · DOE · © CROWN COPYRIGHT

This was how West Malling looked on 19 August 1966. A particularly fine shot taken by the RAF. *DoE*

both war and peacetime, which served at the airfield. These were cut into the granite using the latest state of the art laser stone cutting equipment. The fourth panel depicts the first and last aircraft to serve at West Malling those being the Westland Lysander and the Gloster Javelin. Standing proud over the panels is a bronze statue of an airman in full fighter flying gear running to the scramble.

An unveiling and dedication ceremony was held on Sunday 9 June 2002. Unveiling the various tablets were Air Chief Marshal Sir Christopher Foxley Norris GCB OBE DSO MA, Air Chief Marshal Sir Lewis Hodges KCB CBE DSO and BAR DFC and Bar, Group Captain John Cunningham CBE DSO DFC AE DL, Sir John Stanley MP for Tonbridge and Malling and finally Mr John Loder FRAeS-Ex 29 Squadron West Malling. Bad weather prevented an appearance of the Grace Spitfire Mark 9 although a spirited display by a Tiger Moth from the Tiger Club at Headcorn flown by Chris Jesson bought the afternoon to a closure. A gesture from the Hillreed building company later saw a small memorial placed in Townsend Square reminding the residents that a past commanding officer was Group Captain Peter Townsend, he of royal fame.

Today very little remains to remind us of RAF West Malling. The control tower is now listed and has been renovated to become a coffee house whilst some of the new roads carry the names of past aviators.

The history and exploits of all who served at this famous wartime airfield lie in files encompassed within the National Archives at Kew. They are free to view and tell the story of an airfield that saw peacetime flying through to war and back to peace again. It is fitting therefore that we remind ourselves of the words spoken by Wing Commander Guy Gibson when he served with No. 29 Squadron at West Malling during those dark days of 1941/42: "Of all the airfields in Great Britain, here, many say (including myself) we have the most pleasant".

WEST MALLING SQUADRONS 1940-1960

3	Typhoon 1 b	14.5.43 to 11.6.43
25	Mosquito NF 36	5.9.46 to 30.9.57
	Vampire NF 10	
	Meteor NF 12 and 14	
26	Westland Lysander 111	8.6.40 to 3.9.40
29	Beaufighter 1f	27.4.41 to 13.5.43
	Beaufighter V 1f	
	Mosquito XIII	1.5.44 to 19.6.44
	Mosquito NF 30	29.10.45 to 30.11.50
	Mosquito NF 36	
32	Hurricane 11b, 11c	4.5.42 to 14.6.42
		7.8.42 to 14.8.42
		20.8.42 to 9.9.42
64	Spitfire Vb	6.9.43 to 25.9.43
66	Spitfire 1	31.10.40 to 7.11.40
80	Spitfire IX	5.7.44 to 29.8.44
	Tempest V	
85	Mosquito XV, XII, XVII	13.5.43 to 1.5.44
	Mosquito XIX	21.7.44 to 29.8.44
	Mosquito NF 36	16.4.47 to 23.9.57
	Meteor NF 11, 12 and 14	
	Javelin FAW 2, 6 and 8	5.8.59 to 8.9.60
91	Spitfire XII, XIV	23.4.44 to 21.7.44
96	Beaufighter V1f	8.11.43 to 20.6.44
	Mosquito XIII	
98	Mosquito B 35	27.9.49 to 7.10.49
		17.4.50 to 12.5.50
124	Spitfire HF VII	20.9.43 to 18.3.44
130	Spitfire V6	4.8.43 to 18.9.43
141	Defiant 1	
153	Meteor NF 12 and 14	28.2.55 to 17.9.57
157	Mosquito XIX	21.7.44 to 28.8.44
234	Spitfire Vb	5.8.43 to 19.9.43

264	Defiant 1	14.4.41 to 1.5.41
274	Spitfire IX	5.7.44 to 17.8.44
	Tempest V	
287	Spitfire XVI	10.9.45 to 13.6.46
316	Mustang III	4.8.44 to 11.8.44
322	Spitfire XIV	20.6.44 to 21.7.44
350	Spitfire Vb	
409	Mosquito XIII	16.5.44 to 19.6.44
410	Mosquito NFII and VI	23.10.43 to 9.11.44
486	Typhoon I	
500	Mosquito NF 30	10.5.46 to 10.3.57
	Meteor F3, F4, F8	
531 (Turbinlite)	Havoc and Boston	7.7.41 to 2.10.42
	with Hurricane IIC	8.10.42 to 25.1.43
567	Spitfire XVI	26.4.46 to 15.6.46
	Vengeance IV	
610	Spitfire XIV	
616	Spitfire VI and VII	18.3.44 to 24.4.44

DETACHMENTS AND UNITS

421 Flight	Hurricane II	31.10.40 to 15.11.40
1426 Enemy Aircraft	Me 109, Me 110, He 111	26.6.42 to 27.7.42
1528 Beam Approach	Airspeed Oxford	22.4.42 to 9.11.42
14 Squadron	Mosquito B XVI	6.9.47 to 10.10.47
255 Squadron	Beaufighter IIF	6.9.41 to 3.3.42
14 Squadron	Mosquito B35	3.3.50 to 9.9.50

STATION COMMANDERS AT WEST MALLING 1940-1960

Station Motto
Portam Custodimus

Wing Commander R. W. K. Stevens	1.7.40
Wing Commander T. B. Prickman	28.7.40
Flying Officer F. A. Lewis	18.8.40
Flight Lieutenant V. Mercer Smith	25.8.40
Wing Commander A. M. Wilkinson DSO	14.3.41
Wing Commander S. C. Widdows DFC	14.6.41
Wing Commander V. J. Wheeler MC, DFC	25.6.42
Wing Commander C. M. Wight-Boycott DSO	30.12.42
Wing Commander P. W. Townsend DSO, DFC	25.1.43
Wing Commander T. N. Hayes DSO, DFC	18.6.43
Wing Commander J. A. O'Neil DFC	1.2.44
Squadron Leader G. T. Block	24.11.44
Squadron Leader H. Baxter MM	9.3.45
Wing Commander A. Ingle DFC, AFC	3.10.45
Wing Commander M. G. F. Pedley DSO, OBE, AFC	1.11.46
Wing Commander D. S. Wilson-Macdonald DSO, DFC	26.1.48
Wing Commander H. S. Darley DSO	2.2.48
Group Captain J. Worral DFC	19.4.48
Group Captain H. N. G. Ramsbottom Isherwood DFC, AFC	9.7.49
Group Captain H. S. Darley DSO	12.6.50
Group Captain E. W. Whitley DSO, DFC	18.7.52
Group Captain P. R. Walker DSO, DFC	8.9.52
Group Captain P. H. Hamley AFC	7.8.53
Group Captain G. V. Fryer OBE, AFC	28.11.55
Group Captain E. G. L. Millington DFC	1.11.56
Squadron Leader J. Davis AFC	24.2.58
Wing Commander F. N. Brinsden	2.3.59
Group Captain C. Foxley-Norris DSO	4.8.59
Wing Commander F. N. Brinsden	1.7.60
	until 1.1.61

ACKNOWLEDGEMENTS

I acknowledge with grateful thanks all the people and organisations who have assisted me in the writing of this history.

Anthony Cronk (Landowner — West Malling); C. A. Bryant (Pilot); F. A. Brinton (26 squadron); Reg Kemp (The Manor House); A. K. Robinson (Malling Aero Club); Bernard R. King; F. C. W. Trigg; J. F. F. Lathbury; William Smith; Len Pilkington; Tony Moor; David Collyer; Ken Packham (Metair); Roger Luscombe (Metair); Kent Messenger; Public Record Office; Imperial War Museum; RAF Museum — Hendon; KAHRS Archives; After the Battle; Metair Aircraft Equipment Ltd; Kent County Council; MAP.

To all those that I have forgotten to mention I humbly apologise. My last thanks must go to my wife Barbara for proof reading my work.

BIBLIOGRAPHY

Enemy Coast Ahead — Guy Gibson.
Nightfighter — J. R. D. Braham.
Nightfighter — C. F. Rawnsley and Robert Wright.
Aircraft of the Royal Air Force — Owen Thetford.
The Squadrons of the RAF — James J. Halley.
The Fighter Pilots — Edward H. Sims.
Battle for Britain — Wing Commander H. R. 'Dizzy' Allen DFC.
Duel of Eagles — Peter Townsend.
Private Flying for Leisure and Pleasure — W. Van Essen.
Fighter Squadrons of the RAF — J. D. Rawlings.